Corruption and Economic Growth

About the Authors:

B.K. Chaturvedi served as Member, Planning Commission of India (2007-2014) and of Thirteenth Finance Commission (2007-2009). Starting his career in the Indian Administrative Service (IAS) in 1966, he rose to the highest position in the Civil Service of the country when he was appointed Cabinet Secretary; and he worked in that capacity for three years. He has experience of functioning of government at different levels for more than four decades. He has been Secretary to the Government of India in several Ministries, including Finance, Human Resource Development Petroleum & Natural Gas for more than six years. He was also a member of the board of UNDP and UNICEF. In 2010 one of India's highest civilian awards Padma Bhushan was conferred on him by the President of India.

Shekhar Chandra is an Engineer by training and did his BTech from G.B. Pant University in Uttar Pradesh and then two Masters, one each from Indian Institute of Science, Bangalore, and Georgia Institute of Technology, Atlanta, GA. He has been working at the intersection of economic growth and environment, especially researching India's role in international climate negotiations by combining his analysis of domestic energy challenges with an analysis of the international negotiations, and in particular how India can achieve a fair deal without derailing the process.

Corruption and Economic Growth

B.K. Chaturvedi
Shekhar Chandra

ACADEMIC FOUNDATION
NEW DELHI

www.academicfoundation.org
www.academicfoundation.com

First published in 2015
by

ACADEMIC FOUNDATION
4772-73 / 23 Bharat Ram Road, (23 Ansari Road),
Darya Ganj, New Delhi - 110 002 (India).
Phones : 23245001 / 02 / 03 / 04.
Fax : +91-11-23245005.
E-mail : books@academicfoundation.com
www.academicfoundation.org
www.academicfoundation.com

Cataloging in Publication Data--DK
Courtesy: D.K. Agencies (P) Ltd. <docinfo@dkagencies.com>

Chaturvedi, B. K., author.
Corruption and economic growth / B.K. Chaturvedi, Shekhar Chandra.
pages cm
Includes bibliographical references (pages).
ISBN 9789332701748

1. Corruption--India. 2. Corruption. 3. Corruption--Economic aspects--India. 4. Corruption--Economic aspects. 5. Economic development--India. 6. Economic development. 7. Corruption--Prevention--Government policy--India. I. Shekhar, Chandra, author. II. Title.

DDC 364.1323 23

Typeset by Italics India, New Delhi.

Printed and bound by The Book Mint, New Delhi.
www.thebookmint.in

Dedicated to my grandchildren
Nikita and Dhruv
Who gave me immense joy!

CONTENTS

Acknowledgements

This book is a result of study on corruption over a period of three years at the Planning Commission. During this period, issue of corruption moved to the centre of national debate with reports of Comptroller and Auditor General (CAG) indicating large-scale corruption in allocation of natural resources. An awakened civil society now demanded tougher laws to fight corruption. We found merit in this view but felt that the problem needed a more in-depth treatment. We, therefore, decided to fully explore and understand the reasons for large-scale corruption and ecosystem of the society that would give a comprehensive understanding of the problem.

Several people helped us in understanding the complex issues involved in the work. One of the most critical dimension of the problem was the concept of corruption itself. We benefited immensely with discussions and philosophical insights especially on ethical aspects of corruption given by Dr Vibha Chaturvedi. She looked at some of the problems with more humane perspective. We found this a refreshing change from normal approaches. We found the insights provided by Shri M.L. Sharma, former Special Director, Central Bureau of Investigation (CBI), extremely useful especially in understanding some of the recent changes in laws on corruption. We are very grateful to both of them for improving our understanding of the subject.

Tarun Deep and Krishna Rao helped us with preparation of the draft. P. Sankar provided us support with references. We would like to thank them profusely for this.

Authors

Preface

The book *Corruption and Economic Growth* was conceived when, as Member, Planning Commission, I was working on governance sectors policies for India's Twelfth Five Year Plan. I had experienced the all-pervading nature of corruption four decades back while working as collector in Azamgarh, a district with huge poverty but more in news in last few years for terrorist activity. During subsequent years of my professional life, the problem of corruption continued to be a key issue of governance reforms. Before I took over as Cabinet Secretary, Prime Minister Dr Manmohan Singh had asked me about the nature of administrative reforms required. I recall telling him about the sharp erosion of faith of the people in honesty of All India Services. Later, as I looked at governance scene in India and why a number of states were doing badly both in creating wealth for their citizens and the quality of services being provided to them, corruption emerged as an important and key driver. When Shekhar started assisting me at the Planning Commission after his graduation from United States (US), I asked him to research on various dimensions of corruption. We used both qualitative and quantitative approaches to study why some of the major economies have been successful in creating a more honest society.

When we looked at the issue more closely, I realised that the perception that corruption was holding up growth of poor economies was only half the truth. Corruption had two dimensions: economic and moral. I wanted to hence study a number of questions: Is corruption a moral issue or an economic issue? Or is it both? How does corruption impact different economies? Does it affect equally high income countries and low income countries? Can economic growth and consequent increase in per capita income and quality of life by itself reduce corruption? Was the impact of increase in per capita income on corruption uniform at all income levels? When was the increase more clearly related to reduced corruption? These were questions I wanted answers to. This gradually took me to several related issues which required study. It was important to consider the experience of some global economies which had been successful in reducing corruption. Considering the size of the Indian nation and its economy, low per capita incomes and Westminster model of our democracy, it was also necessary to look at comparable economies and their experiences. We, therefore, chose Singapore, Hong Kong, Finland and the US.

The US was the obvious choice if we wanted to study the comparative systems since size and nature of economies was comparable. Finland selected itself as it had done extremely well on corruption index and has several unique features which needed a detailed look. Two other economies chosen by us, while small in respect of size and population and complexity of problems, had done exceedingly well in reducing corruption and figured very high on all corruption indices. Every agency has applauded their highly successful effort in tackling corruption. Their strategies, though similar in several respects, are distinct. We decided to have a look at these.

As we studied the international experience, one factor which struck us was the inevitability of political corruption or grand corruption. We found that petty corruption, which referred to bribes demanded by officials for delivery of services which the government was expected to provide, was present globally. Yet, in most developed economies, its impact was marginal. Most of these countries had been able to get rid of this in their governance system. Political corruption, however, which could also be called large-scale corruption and has its roots in powerful politicians and senior civil servants supported by corrupt business leaders working in collusion, was in existence in all the countries irrespective of their income levels. We wanted to find its extent in some economies and policies required to control it. We chose the US, Italy and Brazil to know details of some specific cases. We also looked at the history of corruption in Hong Kong.

There were a number of questions cropping up as we went about the above job. We found a need to identify various factors impacting corruption and economic growth. We wanted to measure the impact of increase in corruption on economic growth. This was done through a cross-country study following Mauro who was the pioneer in this field. New data now had become available from Transparency International, in public domain, to measure corruption. It was easily accessible and was for a large number of countries. As against 67 countries for which data were available from Business International (BI) in 1980s, the data covered more than 160 countries. We also had data sourced from the World Bank on governance issues in which corruption was one of the components. We used all this to measure impact of corruption on economic growth and per capita income. We also estimated how much economic growth would be impacted if corruption levels were to reduce to zero or to world average levels. We did this analysis for a select group of countries. Results showed that economy in India would grow up faster by about 2.0 per cent during 1996-2012 and average per capita income would go up three times if corruption were to reduce to the level of Scandinavian countries. We, however, also found that low incomes imposed a boundary beyond which global economies had failed to reduce corruption. Such a boundary kept on expanding as incomes went up. This restricted the abilities of countries to reduce corruption to within a certain range.

While we studied these questions, the Anna Hazare movement against corruption was gaining strength. A Gandhian, a highly dedicated and selfless social worker, Anna had been able to unite the country's youth in his fight against corruption. He raised a demand for setting up Lokpal to enquire into corruption against high public officials, including politicians and ministers. He strongly focused on creation of an independent institution for investigating cases of corruption against the political executive and civil servants. He wanted it to be independent of the government. As the battle was going on, we realised that we must have a detailed look at the Indian scene too. A lot has been written about corruption in India. The Second Administrative Reforms Commission in its fourth report on Ethics in Governance had looked at corruption in India and given its recommendations. The government was reviewing it and considering how these could be implemented. It was, however, clear to us that efforts in this direction had been completely inadequate. The past history of the enactment of the Lokpal Bill covering a period of more than four decades showed that there was no political will across the major political parties to frame such a law. In the past, this had led to failure in enacting such a law. We realised that people were very harassed both by petty and political corruption in the country. We, therefore, decided to have a look at the Lokpal Act as it had emerged after the discussions in the Parliament and approval by the President. We found that there were voices both for and against the present act. Considering that a lot of petty corruption is in the domain of states, there was nothing in the bill about it, except a clause advising setting of Lokayukta in each state within a period of one year. Even a template was avoided about what the contours of such a Lokayukta should be. We also felt worried about a complete lack of comprehensive strategy on the issue of fighting corruption. We felt that education, prevention and enforcement or punishment should be the essential ingredients of such a comprehensive plan. We, therefore, considered the changes in the act consistent with the above approach so that corruption could be fought more effectively in the country. While we considered the above ideas, we were conscious that economic growth had a major impact on levels of corruption. No strategy to fight corruption could be prepared without including economic growth as a key driver for reducing corruption.

As we worked on all these areas, there was one thought which was with us all along. This related to the concept of corruption itself along with its measurement. We had initially accepted the concept of corruption as understood by United Nations (UN) agencies, Transparency International and World Bank. We, however, realised that there were large gaps in this concept of corruption and it needed to be focused on. The problems of private sectors corruption had emerged in the recent decade and many countries had not realised it adequately. There was no reflection of this in their laws. There were other gaps too. We decided, therefore, to start the book with the concept of corruption including its ethical dimensions. While doing this, we assumed the measurement methodology of Transparency International and World Bank, as these covered very large sets of data.

The book has seven chapters. Chapter 1 deals with the concept of corruption and its measurement. Chapter 2 deals with corruption and economic growth. It gives details of work done earlier in this field starting with Paulo Mauro, identifies factors which could explain cross-country variation in growth, and works out impact of increase or decrease in corruption index on GDP (gross domestic product) growth, as well as on per capita income. We study the period 1996-2012 using data for 147 countries. The chapter also includes a country-wise impact of decrease in corruption on GDP growth and per capita incomes in some select group of economies with high level of corruption. Chapter 3 deals with factors impacting corruption. It identifies various factors which influence level of corruption in a country and the extent of such an impact. It also studies whether the explanatory variables identified by us are an adequate explanation in the context of cross country variation in corruption. We use data for nearly 150 countries during this study. Chapter 4 deals with international experience in the field of corruption control and its elimination. We give details of the UN convention against corruption and experience of the US, Finland, Singapore and Hong Kong. We also mention details of several cases of political corruption in the US, Italy and Brazil to illustrate how politicians and senior executives of companies have been a part of it. This highlights the difficulty in controlling it. Chapter 5 deals with fighting corruption with a focus on economic growth and highlights how income levels limit the ability of a country to reduce corruption. As incomes grow, nations become stronger and more capable to reduce corruption. We analyse this sensitivity at different income levels and find that at per capita incomes of $4,000-5,000 (i.e. when economies transition into upper middle income zone), the impact of increased income on corruption is more significant. Prior to it, the decline in corruption is governed by other policy interventions of governments. We highlight the importance of developing a good ecosystem to reduce corruption. We also give a detailed strategy for fighting corruption built around economic growth. Chapter 6 deals with the Indian scene. We mention here the history of corruption in India starting with *Arthashastra* and then describe some major cases of corruption in the last six decades. We then consider some studies on the extent of corruption in India, impact of economic reforms and faster growth on emergence of new areas of corruption and current policies on reducing corruption. We finally suggest a comprehensive approach to tackling corruption and developing an honest society by 2030. Chapter 7 gives conclusions of the study and briefly mentions the extent of corruption, international experience and how India can become an honest society with a good quality of life.

So, here is this book which evolved as a result of the above thoughts.

B.K. Chaturvedi
New Delhi.

1

Corruption

Concept and Measurement

Corruption has been a major concern globally for quite some time. It has been at the centre of intense public discourse in India for last 6-7 years and was a major political issue in the parliamentary elections in 2014. Before undertaking any discussion on corruption in general or in the Indian context, it is worthwhile to understand what is meant by corruption. The conceptual contours of this word, which we use so frequently, have relevance not only for a clearer understanding of the term but also have implications for policy measures to fight corruption.

The Oxford English Dictionary mentions several different senses of corruption.[1] In one sense, it applies to objects and signifies some kind of degeneration, decomposition, putrefaction, spoiling of quality, adulteration, etc. In the case of language, it signifies change in the original meaning of a word, which is erroneous or debased. When used for taste it means debasement. It is also used for computer data and signifies alteration or error. These senses are not relevant for us here. In the context of human actions, it signifies 'dishonest or fraudulent conduct' by persons in positions of power. Bribery is a typical example of corruption. The term corruption is also used for moral depravity, moral debasement or diminution of a person's moral virtues. In its most common use, it means 'misuse of public office for personal gain'.[2] Our focus would primarily be on its use in the context of human actions. When we use the term in the context of governments, corporations, institutions and institutional processes, it is a derivative use and refers either to corrupt deeds of functionaries of that institution or to the fact that the processes have not been carried out in an honest manner.

Not all cases of corruption necessarily involve public office or even an institutional role. Officials in private institutions or organisations like firms, companies, corporations and stock exchanges can also indulge in corruption. Moreover, sometimes a person may indulge in corruption in a purely private capacity; for example, when a citizen misuses his or her voting right for financial or other kind of gain. In most debates on corruption, however, it is the misuse of political or governmental office that remains the focal concern. Still corruption by private institutions or individuals cannot be ignored. Corruption can be of various kinds: political, economic, social or moral. It is also quite clear that people's perceptions about corrupt actions differ across societies. The same activity may be considered corrupt in one society but may be alright in another. Giving gifts of value to government officials on certain occasions is customary in some places, but in others it is perceived as corruption. During Mughal reign in India, such gifts were considered a courtesy and this practice continued during British Raj and is prevalent even today. What is considered as corrupt depends to some extent on socio-cultural factors.

It seems thus that a strict definition of 'corruption' in terms of its necessary and sufficient conditions is not feasible. It does not seem possible to point out some feature(s), which can be said to constitute corruption and must be shared by every instance of corruption. Corrupt actions include acts of commission, as well as acts of omission. Therefore, a strict definition cannot be given, which will cover all different kinds of corruption and all different senses of the term. It appears that here we have what Wittgenstein (1973) calls a 'family resemblance' concept, where every instance of corruption will share some features with some other instances of corruption, although there is no feature which will be shared by all the instances.[3] It is important to recognise that all cases of corruption are not legal offences. For example, tipping a bearer in advance to obtain a good place in a restaurant, giving gifts to high officials or politically powerful people on festivals and other important occasions, funding holidays of family members of highly placed officials, using political or bureaucratic connections to secure admission for one's child through discretionary quotas in institutions, exerting pressure on selection processes through recommendations by influential people, etc., may not always fall into the category of legal offences. Similarly, donations to social-service organisations run by highly placed government officials are not always illegal. Giving gifts of value to highly placed officials is also sometimes not considered as corrupt and illegal. The basic test, which ought to be applied in all such cases is whether such transactions result in lowering the confidence of people in fairness of government systems or not.

The most widely used and dominant sense of the word corruption remains 'misuse of a public office for personal gain.' The two operative words here are 'misuse' and 'personal gain'. What is meant by 'misuse'? If someone uses a public office dishonestly for personal gain rather than for the institutional purpose behind it, it constitutes misuse. Typically an official taking a bribe to tweak an institutional process will be a case of misuse. There can be other instances where the misuse is clear. But in some cases, it may not be clear whether it is misuse or not. Does delaying or obstructing some process of decision making constitute misuse? Similarly one may ask whether failure to follow some procedural norms amounts to corruption. The crucial factor here seems to be the question of personal gain. If these activities are prompted by the motive of personal gain and actually result in personal gain, the person's actions will be regarded as corrupt. Since one person cannot know with certainty the motives behind someone else's actions, the real test lies in the actual presence of or attempts made to have personal gain. A delay in taking decisions may be due to laziness or an over-cautious approach or indecisive nature of the concerned official. Similarly failure to follow rules or procedural norms may be prompted by laziness, carelessness, apathy or even by enthusiasm to finish the job fast. Such cases, when not accompanied by personal gain for the concerned agent, cannot be said to constitute corrupt actions. It is for this reason that a distinction has to be made between a bona fide mistake and negligence on the one hand and a corrupt action on the other. Suppose no personal gain accrues to the agent in question, but his or her failure to follow rules results in some financial loss to the institution to which the agent belongs. In our opinion in this case also, the action cannot be called corrupt unless bad faith or malfeasance is established. Such actions fall in the definition of negligence in performing one's responsibility. As already said, actual personal gain or attempts to have it is the acid-test, which distinguishes a corrupt action from a non-corrupt one. Mere intention of personal gain would not suffice.[4] (Please see detailed definitions as to what constitutes corruption in some of the countries mentioned later in the chapter.)

The personal gain can be in various forms. Most commonly it is in the form of economic gain, like money, property, etc., but it can also be in the form of political power, career advancement or some other gain. In many cases of corruption, the motivation is not economic gain, but other kinds of gain. For example, researchers or academicians may plagiarise for increasing publications, students may cheat in examinations to get good results or gain entry into a sought after programme, or an official may violate the confidentiality of an examination paper to oblige a friend. In most cases, corruption does involve breaking of some rules or procedural norms. However in some cases, this may not be so. We know that sometimes a bribe can be demanded or given for expediting some decision, which is in conformity with the rules and is a correct decision. Bardhan (1997) mentions that in Russia, a clear distinction is made between illegal gratification for a decision in accordance with rules and for a decision against the rules.[5] It is well known that bribes are demanded and given for releasing due payments and expediting decisions. In India, for example, people often complain of such corruption with regard to many public services like passport office, transport authorities, development authorities and funding agencies.

We would like to emphasise that corruption is primarily a moral issue and not merely an economic, political, social or governance issue. Corrupt actions are morally undesirable. This is supported by the general use of the word corruption and its derivatives. A corrupt action signifies a dishonest one, a corrupt person means a dishonest and unscrupulous one and a corrupt society represents a morally depraved one. Meaning of 'dishonest or unscrupulous' can only be understood in relation to the value system of a society and may vary with variations in values across cultures. However, it remains true that basic moral values of different cultures are similar to a great extent. Dishonesty, for example, is held to be unethical everywhere. Most discussions on corruption confine themselves to economic corruption and analyse it primarily in terms of its economic consequences or issues of governance affecting economic activity. It is very important to acknowledge that corruption is primarily a moral issue. This does not mean that economic dimensions of corruption are not important, but we need to emphasise that our abhorrence of corruption is based upon our moral values. Even if corruption can be shown to have beneficial economic consequences or increased efficiency in some cases, such considerations do not offer a moral justification of corruption.

Can we say that all corrupt actions fall in the category of ethically wrong actions? Most people would agree that it is true in case of most corrupt actions but not all. One may argue that a corrupt action done for a noble cause is not unethical. For example, suppose a bribe is given to an official of a repressive regime to save the life of a popular leader or to get a noble person facing execution out of the prison or to save someone from torture or to secure valuable information to promote national interest. One may argue that in these cases, bribing cannot be said to be unethical. This is a difficult issue. One is reminded of such cases during the Second World War in order to save Jews from persecution by Nazis. However, the moral judgement in such cases depends on the judgement that the cause in question is noble and the person being helped deserves to be saved. Suppose one bribes an official to enable a criminal to get away from prison; we will not regard it as a good action. People may evaluate persons and causes differently and may lead to different moral judgements with respect to an instance of the kind mentioned above. We know how opinions differ in case of revolutionaries or leaders of mass movements against the establishment. There is a difference of opinion among ethical philosophers on the question whether corruption for a noble cause is ethically desirable or not. Those who believe like Mahatma Gandhi that means to a good goal should also be pure will regard such acts also as unethical. However, those who believe that ends justify means may regard such actions as right provided they approve of the end. It is not possible here to go into a debate on the issue of ends and means. It suffices to say that even in supposed cases of corruption for a noble cause, ethicality of the actions in question remains controversial.

Moreover even if we admit that corruption in such cases is morally acceptable, it only applies to a very small number of exceptions.

It is often mentioned that corruption has existed in all societies from the early years of civilisation.[6] This, however, does not provide a justification for corruption. Even if corruption has existed for a long time, it does not follow that every nation and every society should not work towards minimising corruption. When people in a society no longer feel morally repulsed by wide-spread corruption, it leads to a general decline in the moral standards of people. Wherever corruption is widespread, social disapproval of corruption is weak and legal action against corruption is not quick and efficient, we find that people have a greater tendency to resort to corruption.[7] Tolerance of corruption in a society ultimately leads to an environment where people do not place value on following rules and norms. Such a society can neither progress economically nor socially and is not conducive to the general well-being of its members.

Let us now focus on corrupt actions involving misuse of a public office for personal gain. These are intentional actions prompted by a motive of personal gain. The most obvious examples of corruption are bribery and nepotism. Let us take the example of bribery to discuss some conceptual issues. An action of bribing has several dimensions: there is more than one agent, effect of bribing on the concerned institution or its processes, its effect on the agents, agents' moral responsibility and liability for punishment. Each of these aspects gives rise to certain issues. Suppose a government official accepts a bribe to oblige a contractor by disclosing to him the quotations submitted by other applicants for undertaking a construction project. This gives the contractor an unfair advantage by enabling him to adjust his or her quotations with a view to win the contract. Who is the corruptor in this case, the person who demands and accepts a bribe or also the person who gives the bribe? The official is misusing his or her public office for personal financial gain. Obviously, the person is guilty of corruption. The person who gives the bribe is not holding a public office. However, he initiates a process for his own personal gain, which corrupts the institutional processes. It seems to us that both are corruptors. When corruption by public officials is discussed, very often the bribe-giver is looked at merely as a victim. However, we cannot overlook that the bribe-giver is also a corruptor, even if his or her culpability may be less in some situations. Secondly, both the bribe-giver and the bribe-taker get corrupted in this process, as do the institutional processes; the agents because their moral character is diminished in the process, institutional processes because they are vitiated and the institutional purposes get compromised. Thus, a corrupt action has detrimental effects on the concerned agents as well as the institution. There may be a counter view that the bribe-giver is not corrupted, especially if the person never offers a bribe in future. Suppose the single corrupt action fills the person with tremendous shame and he or she vows to only take the straight path in future. One may argue that the action of bribing here has an ennobling effect on the person. We do not agree with this conclusion. Granted that a corrupt action may generate different emotional responses in different agents, it still remains true that giving of bribe was motivated by an unethical objective and the agent intentionally resorted to an unethical action. Therefore, it can be said that bribing has a corrupting effect on the agent here. In our view, every corrupt action results in some sort of weakening of one's moral character. Of course, repeated corrupt actions will lead to further diminution. Definitions of corruption in many countries mentioned later do seem to acknowledge the culpability of the bribe-giver.

In the above example, some procedural rule or norm is broken by the public official. In most cases of corruption, this is likely to be so. People offer bribe to get something done, when it is not permissible under the existing rules. Bribes can also be offered when one wants a decision to be expedited. If one offers a bribe to a public official with the specific purpose of getting a favourable decision against rules, culpability of the person cannot be overlooked or excused. Even if a bribe is offered for getting something done which is very essential or urgent, the culpability remains, though mitigating circumstances are there. Suppose one offers a bribe to an official for obtaining some medicine, which is rationed and in short supply and is required urgently to save the life of his child. While most of us will have sympathy for the bribe-giver here, it remains a case of bribery. The culpability of the person who takes the bribe is of course obvious. In examples where a bribe is demanded and given for expediting a correct decision, culpability of the bribe-giver does not seem so obvious. The bribe-giver is placed in a difficult situation for no fault of his or her. Can we say here also that the bribe-giver is culpable? Similarly we can imagine situations which may raise doubts about the culpability of the one who accepts a bribe. Suppose one takes bribes but uses these to support a good cause. Is the bribe-taker still a corruptor and corrupted? Such thought experiments do raise questions difficult to answer and will have an impact on our moral assessment of the agents and their actions. However, culpability of the bribe-giver and the bribe-taker cannot be denied even in such examples. Therefore, both the bribe-giver and the person accepting the bribe are morally responsible, both are corruptors and both are corrupted. This would be more readily conceded where the bribe-giver's motivation is to get an undue favour and the bribe-taker's motivation is personal gain. In some cases, where strong mitigating considerations are present, the judgement may differ. However both persons are morally responsible, though the degree of culpability may vary. The issue of moral responsibility in case of nepotism seems to be different. Suppose, one gets a job as a result of favour from a highly placed relative in the form of influencing the selection process. The one who exercises pressure on the process of selection to secure a job for one's relative is obviously guilty of corruption. One may argue that the one who receives the favour is neither a corruptor nor corrupted. In case the favour was not done because of a request by this person or the person remains oblivious of the pressure exercised by the concerned relative, it does seem that the recipient of the favour has no moral responsibility for the corrupt action. But in a case of nepotism where both parties play an active role, both parties are morally responsible. It is a separate matter what the law of the land says about culpability of the parties. The examples of bribery and nepotism show that cases of different kinds of corruption may exhibit important differences, and these need to be taken into account. It is to be noted that an action may be considered corrupt within an institutional setting, though in itself it may not be so considered. For example, under normal circumstances, it is alright if a person, who is good in analysing and anticipating share market, or has happened to overhear a conversation between two persons about the rise in share prices of a certain commodity, offers a tip to a close friend. But in an institutional setting, sharing information about the shares of a company or corporation with somebody else will constitute insider trading and may be a legal offence. Similarly making a recommendation in someone's favour may be alright by itself but within an institutional setting may amount to nepotism.

One may ask: what is the criterion for judging corrupt actions as morally undesirable? The answer will depend on the ethical perspective one takes. A deontologist standpoint will argue that it is so because of violation of a duty or obligation. Immanuel Kant, for example, regarded moral principles as commands of reason. He argued that an action is moral, if and only if, it is in conformity with duty and the agent performs it out of respect for duty. In his theory, consequences of the action are irrelevant for the moral worth of that action. Even if a duty performed for duty's sake leads to bad consequences, the action is right. For example, telling the truth and keeping one's promise are right actions and they remain so whatever be the consequences.[8] Regarding examples of corruption for noble cause mentioned earlier, Kant's theory would imply that such actions are wrong. Most ethical philosophers find this rigid standpoint problematic. Apart from the fact that it does not allow any exceptions to a moral principle, it also fails to take into account situations in real life where one is faced with a dilemma because of a conflict between two moral principles. In such situations, it is generally allowed that taking recourse to the lesser evil is alright.

A consequentialist theory regards the moral worth of an action to be determined by its consequences. A well-known example is utilitarianism, which holds that an action is right, if and only if, it leads to the greatest happiness of the greatest numbers. Here, the intention of the agent is irrelevant.[9] Some forms of utilitarianism do recognise that our general moral principles have been formulated in order to promote general happiness, and therefore, an agent need not calculate the consequences before undertaking each action. So long as one acts in conformity with well-established moral principles, it is alright. Utilitarianism also faces difficulties and has been criticised by several thinkers including John Rawls and Amartya Sen.

It is not within the purview of this discussion to undertake a detailed discussion of the merits and demerits of these and other ethical theories. The limited objective is to clarify that different kinds of grounds can be given to justify why corrupt actions are morally undesirable depending upon the ethical theory being accepted. It may be noted that the moral evaluation of a specific action may be the same under different theories. However, sometimes different theories may take a very different view on the moral evaluation of an action. Supposed instances of corruption for a noble cause illustrate this point well. For example, suppose the people in an area will benefit enormously if a dam is constructed on the river in that area. The concerned officials, however, are demanding a hefty bribe to give the required clearances. The political representative of the area decides to pay that bribe in the larger interest by collecting funds from many wealthy people. A deontologist like Kant would regard the action as wrong despite its good consequences. A utilitarian may allow that the action is right under those circumstances. Generally speaking, however, we find an agreement among different ethical theories regarding the rightness of specific actions.[10]

We would like to argue that corrupt actions in general are morally undesirable even if in some cases a corrupt action leads to some beneficial consequences for a large group of people. In some exceptional cases, it may be justified as choosing a lesser evil where circumstances do not permit a better choice. Such examples, however, do not admit of an easy answer and remain problematic. The fact that corruption in general has harmful effects of various kinds, including economic ones, is uncontroverted. Many studies have pointed out such effects. From a holistic point of view, corruption is not beneficial for a society in the long run, even if it may give short-term economically beneficial consequences in some cases. Prevalence of and tolerance for corruption ultimately leads to moral deterioration of the social environment, which in turn is detrimental to human well-being.

Defining Corruption

Most countries have laws defining what constitutes corruption and specifically bribery. As mentioned earlier, we follow the broad concept of 'use of public office for private gains.' There are some variations, however, amongst them. In the recent times, one of the major developments in this field has been inclusion of corruption in private companies. The definition of United Nations Development Programme (UNDP) on bribery has accordingly undergone a change. While earlier, UNDP considered corruption as "misuse of public power, office or authority for private benefit through bribery, extortion, influence paddling, Nepotism, Fraud, Speed money or embezzlement," considering the need for controlling corruption in private sector, the concept now has been modified to "misuse of entrusted power for private gain."[11] The laws of corruption and bribery give a very wide definition of the term. To consider nature and scope of law, we have considered laws in four countries: Singapore, Hong Kong, the US and India. We examined various aspects of laws on this issue in these countries. This included nature of activities considered corrupt, definition of public servant, corruption in private sector, and treatment of bribe-givers and various public officials. We also compared the Indian law on this issue.

The definition of corruption mentioning various actions and nature of benefits received is fairly wide in all the countries. It includes both: acts of commission and acts of omission. It includes any advantage received as inducement or reward for performing or abstaining from performing any act. It covers expediting, hindering, delaying or preventing any act due to above-mentioned inducement. It covers assisting or favouring anybody in respect of transaction of a business with a public body. It includes gifts, fee, commission or any movable or immovable property. It covers employment official position or any other favour. The basic prerequisite in all these laws is that the advantage is related to act of a public official.

In the US, there is a very important widening of this definition. It applies also to all public officials who have been selected for a job but not actually joined. This provision is possibly because in the US, there is a long process of approval for several appointments and there is a large time gap. Presidents and vice presidents take office with some time gap. The Indian definition of corruption is fairly wide and includes acts of commission or of forbearance as well as advantages and favours of all kind. It covers people who are public servants or expecting to be so. It covers persons who obtain some benefits or attempt to obtain it. The nature of benefits is fairly wide and includes both pecuniary and others. It also covers those who obtain gratification or benefit for doing a job which he does not intend or cannot or is not in position to do. The basic requirement is obtaining non-legal remuneration. The definition of corruption in the Indian act compares well with other countries.

The acts on prevention of corruption in these countries apply to official actions of all public servants. It covers all government officials and public body officials under the control of the government. It applies also to ministers and members of the parliament performing any public duty. In Hong Kong, it is specifically mentioned in the act that it applies to chief executive officer, the successor to the governor of the colonial times. In the Singapore act, a specific mention has been made of members of the parliament being covered under it. The US act specifies members of congress, delegates or resident commissioner either before or after such official has qualified or an officer or an employee or persons acting for or on behalf of the US, or any department, agency, or of government thereof. In India too, it has a very wide coverage and includes all officials and others covered by above definition. It specifically mentions corporations, local bodies, educational institutions, judges and officers appointed by them including liquidators and arbitrators. It also covers a very wide class of persons performing a public duty. The word public duty is defined very broadly and includes all duties in the performance of which state or public or community at large has an interest. It specifically does not mention members of the parliament or of state assembly. However, the definition of public duty is so all embracing that the act is applicable to them.

An important provision which is part of most of the laws is the onus of proof if gratification or other benefits are received. In all such cases, it is presumed that the benefit was illegal unless proved otherwise by the beneficiary. This makes it difficult for corrupt officials and facilitates their conviction.

In all countries, laws make no distinction between a bribe-giver and persons accepting bribe. Both are considered equally liable. In the UN Convention Against Corruption (UNCAC), similar provision has been suggested.[12] Laws of most countries follow this. In India, however, the person offering bribe is considered an abettor and punished accordingly. A provision in the act makes statements given by him a special protection. The act prohibits its use against him. This needs change to bring it in conformity with international practice.

Corruption in private sector has been a cause of concern globally as most of the investment is made by private players. Hong Kong has made it punishable in its anti-bribery ordinance. Since the country had been a hub of financial sector activities, it was necessary to ensure confidence of investors to make a law providing for punishment to corrupt employees of private sector companies. Similar provision already exists in Singapore anti-corruption act. The Second Administrative Reforms Commission (ARC) of India, however, considered this and did not recommend any change in law to include corruption in private companies within the ambit of the act. The reasons were two fold. First, the Companies Act in India had several provisions which took care of such corrupt acts. Second, the Articles of Association of companies can provide for action in such cases. Both these arguments are weak. The protection to companies available from coverage in anti- corruption act of Singapore and Hong Kong is specific, and clear with heavy penalties of up to five years imprisonment to corrupt agents. This is not so under Indian laws. None of the provisions quoted by ARC can provide the same degree of comfort to private companies.

Corruption Prevention Act, 1988, the Indian law on corruption, has provisions for criminal misconduct by public servants.[13] This needs a review. The nature of offences included in the misconduct are covered by other earlier sections where getting any favours apart from legal remuneration has been made a criminal offence. To make it amply clear, it can be clarified that such remuneration can be for public servant himself or procured by him for others. This must however involve obtaining some advantage by him which is not a legal remuneration but in addition to it. There have also been a lot of concerns on Section 13(1)(d)(iii) of the act which reads as follows: "if he while holding office as a public servant obtains for any person any valuable thing or pecuniary advantage without any public interest, he is guilty of criminal misconduct and liable for punishment."

These provisions are quite unlike any other act on this issue in other countries. The law suffers from several defects. First, it does not distinguish between bona fide and mala fide act of civil servants. Second, public interest is not defined. Third, it does not consider whether any advantage has accrued to the public servant or even likely to accrue at any stage. It finds him guilty irrespective of that. There is a need to bring a law consistent with the principles of justice so that only that advantage or favour or benefit which is not a legal remuneration is punishable. There is a need to repeal the above provision from the purview of the act.

The laws of different countries defining corruption show a similarity. The definition of public servant is fairly wide and covers both government officials and political executives and members of legislatures. The presumption is against accused persons and the onus is on them to prove that certain benefits which they got were legal. On bribe-giver being guilty and corruption in private sector, the Indian laws are different and need review. These also need to be changed on several issues relating to criminal misconduct.

Measurement of Corruption

Measurement of corruption is a difficult task. Earlier, authors have depended on this for the work done by Business International (BI) now incorporated as Economist Intelligence Unit. The data were collected by them for corruption and other indices for use of banks, corporations and other large international players. It had been used by Mauro, who was the pioneer in the field of cross-country analysis of corruption. It was available at that time for 68 countries for 56 country risk factors for the period 1980-1983.[14] It was also available for 57 countries, which were assessed on 30 country risk factors, for the period 1971-1979. These data were available on payment and there was a market for it. However since 1995, Transparency International (TI) started preparing the index on corruption. This index is in fact a poll of polls. It is based on indices prepared by several agencies. Corruption perception index for 2013 is based on data obtained from 13 agencies. Each one of them has developed the index based on materials compiled by them from their own sources. The agencies are as follows:

(a) African Development Bank Governance Ratings 2012.
(b) Bertelsmann Foundation Sustainable Governance Indicators 2014.
(c) Bertelsmann Foundation Transformation Index 2014.
(d) Economist Intelligence Unit Country Risk Ratings.
(e) Freedom House Nations in Transit 2013.
(f) Global Insight Country Risk Ratings.
(g) IMD World Competitiveness Yearbook 2013.
(h) Political and Economic Risk Consultancy Asian Intelligence 2013.
(i) Political Risk Services International Country Risk Guide.
(j) Transparency International Bribe Payers Survey 2011.
(k) World Bank—Country Policy and Institutional Assessment 2012.
(l) World Economic Forum Executive Opinion Survey (EOS) 2013.
(m) World Justice Project Rule of Law Index 2013.

The other source of data on corruption measurement is the World Bank. These data too are freely available and is in public domain. It compares quite well with the TI data. The data sources used by the World Bank are for preparing a World Bank governance indicator. These indicators cover six areas based on which the governance index is prepared. These include regulatory index, corruption index, political stability, rule of law, government effectiveness and voice and accountability. The corruption index used by us in this study, except where indicated, is the one which is prepared by the World Bank. The governance indicators are based on following four different types of data sources:

(a) Surveys of households and firms from 9 data sources including the Afro Barometer Surveys, Gallup World Poll and Global Competitiveness Report survey.
(b) Commercial business information providers from 9 data sources including the Economist Intelligence Unit, Global Insight and Political Risk Services.
(c) Non-governmental organisations from 11 data sources including Global Integrity, Freedom House, Reporters Without Borders; and
(d) Public sector organisations from 8 data sources including the CPIA assessment of World Bank and regional development banks, the EBRD Transition Report and French Ministry of Finance Institutional Profiles Database.

We feel that using the two data sources from TI and the World Bank has major advantages. First, it is in public domain. Second, it is available to all researchers freely and, therefore, correctives are possible. Third, the data sources by both are dependent on other data compilation and thus, cover a very wide base. This provides adequate correctives in case of bias from any data source.

Petty Corruption and Political Corruption

While measurement of corruption indicates the degree of its prevalence in the economy, it is broadly identifiable in two classes depending upon the driver of corruption. The petty corruption is demand of bribery or other benefits for delivery of public services provided at grass-roots level. This includes demand of gratification for getting ration cards for PDS (public distribution system), electric connection for households, permission for construction of buildings for houses or industry, registering cases with police stations, fighting cases in courts, getting subsidies from governments, and getting various permissions for registration of vehicles and driving licence etc. There are several other services including getting bank loans, subsidy under plan schemes like Indira Awas Yojna and wages under Mahatma Gandhi National Rural Emplyment Guarantee Act (MNREGA). The hallmark of this type of corruption is that it is small in value and driven primarily by the corrupt civil servants. Given the high level of corruption in many economies, especially low income countries, often the bribe money is shared with local politicians. This provides insurance to the corrupt civil servant against transfer or any action against him if people complain. The sharing ensures that the politician stands up for the civil servant and no action is taken against him.

The main driver of political corruption is the politician himself, though it need not always be the case. Its main characteristic is that it is large in value. It is also referred to as grand corruption. Major tenders, procurement or purchase by government, large value imports or exports, mining concessions given illegally or in violation of norms, benefits to corporates in return for funds, and political donations of large value for getting some concessions are some of the sources of this type of corruption. Rose-Ackerman (1999) has defined this as:[15]

> Grand corruption occurs at highest level of government and involves major Govt. projects and programmes. Government frequently transfers large financial benefits to private firms through procurement contracts and the award of concessions. Bribes transfer monopoly rents to private investors with a share to the corrupted officials Privatisation processes are vulnerable to corrupt inside deals.

Notes and References

1. *http://www.oxforddictionaries.com/definition/english/corruption*
2. Guhan, S. and P. Samuel (1997). *Corruption in India: Agenda.* New Delhi: Vision Books Publication; See also: Bardhan, P. (1997). "Corruption and Development: A Review of Issues", *Journal of Economic Literature* 35(3): 1320-46, September. American Economic Association; *Stanford Encyclopedia of Philosophy*, available at: *http://plato.stanford.edu/entries/corruption/*
3. Wittgenstein, L. (1973). *Philosophical Investigations.* 3rd edition. Pearson Publication.
4. See definitions of corruption in Singapore and Hong Kong:

4.1 Singapore's Prevention of Corruption Act, 1960.

Definition of Corruption: What is commonly known as a 'bribe' is described as a 'corrupt gratification" in the Act. 'Gratifications' can take many forms, and they include:

(a) money or any gift, loan, fee, reward, commission, valuable security or other property or interest in property of any description, whether movable or immovable;

(b) any office, employment or contract;

(c) any payment, release, discharge of liquidation of any loan, obligation or other liability whatsoever, whether in whole or in part;

(d) any other service, favour, advantage of any description whatsoever, including protection from any penalty or disability incurred or apprehended or from any action or proceedings of a disciplinary or penal nature, whether or not already instituted, and including the exercise or the forbearance from the exercise of any right or any official power or duty; or

(e) any offer, undertaking or promise of any gratification within the meaning of paragraphs a, b, c and d.

4.2 Hong Kong Definition of Corruption: The Prevention of Bribery Ordinance (PBO) is the law that combats corruption. It governs both the private and the public sectors.

4.2.1 For public sector, it says:

(a) Any person who, whether in Hong Kong or elsewhere, without lawful authority or reasonable excuse, offers any advantage to a public servant as an inducement to or reward for or otherwise on account of that public servant's;

(b) performing or abstaining from performing, or having performed or abstained from performing, any act in his capacity as a public servant;

(c) expediting, delaying, hindering or preventing, or having expedited, delayed, hindered or prevented, the performance of an act, whether by that public servant or by any other public servant in his or that other public servant's capacity as a public servant; or

(d) assisting, favouring, hindering or delaying, or having assisted, favoured, hindered or delayed, any person in the transaction of any business with a public body, shall be guilty of an offence.

(e) Any public servant who, whether in Hong Kong or elsewhere, without lawful authority or reasonable excuse, solicits or accepts any advantage as an inducement to or reward for or otherwise on account of his: (a) performing or abstaining from performing, or having performed or abstained from performing, any act in his capacity as a public servant; (b) expediting, delaying, hindering or preventing, or having expedited, delayed, hindered or prevented, the performance of an act whether by himself or by any other public servant in his or that other public servant's capacity as a public servant; or (c) assisting, favouring, hindering or delaying, or having assisted, favoured, hindered or delayed, any person in the transaction of any business with a public body, shall be guilty of an offence.

(f) Any person who, whether in Hong Kong or elsewhere, without lawful authority or reasonable excuse, offers any advantage to the Chief Executive as an induce: (a) meant to or reward for or otherwise on account of the Chief Executive's performing or abstaining from performing, or having performed or abstained from performing, any act in his capacity as the Chief Executive; (b) expediting, delaying, hindering or preventing, or having expedited, delayed, hindered or prevented, the performance of an act, whether by the Chief Executive in his capacity as the Chief Executive or by any public servant in his capacity as a public servant; or (c) assisting, favouring, hindering or delaying, or having assisted, favoured, hindered or delayed, any person in the transaction of any business with a public body, shall be guilty of an offence.

(g) If the Chief Executive, whether in Hong Kong or elsewhere, without lawful authority or reasonable excuse, solicits or accepts any advantage as an inducement to or reward for or otherwise on account of his: (a) performing or abstaining from performing, or having performed or abstained from performing, any act in his capacity as the Chief Executive; (b) expediting, delaying, hindering or preventing, or having expedited, delayed, hindered or prevented, the performance of an act, whether by the Chief Executive in his capacity as the Chief Executive or by any public servant in his capacity as a public servant; or (c) assisting, favoring, hindering or delaying, or having assisted, favored, hindered or delayed, any person in the transaction of any business with a public body, he shall be guilty of an offence.

4.2.2. Similar provisions exist for private sector under Section 9 of the act.

5. Bardhan, P. (1997). "Corruption and Development: A Review of Issues", *Journal of Economic Literature* 35(3): 1320-46, September. American Economic Association.

6. We find mention of corruption in ancient thinkers like Aristotle and Kautiliya. See also, Heidenheimer, Arnold J. and Michael Johnston (eds) (2001). *Political Corruption: Concepts and Contexts*. Transaction Publishers. 3rd edition; Kangle, R.P. (1965). *The Kautiliya Arthashastra* (Part I-III). New Delhi: Motilal Banarsidas Publishers.

7. Anderson, J., D. Kaufmann and F. Recanatini (2003). "Service Delivery, Poverty and Corruption: Common Threads from Diagnostic Surveys", Background paper for *World Development Report 2004*. Washington DC: World Bank. June 27. *www.worldbank.org/wbi/governance/capacitybuild/d-surveys.html*

8. Paton, H.J. (1979). *The Moral Law: Kant's Groundwork of The Metaphysic of Morals*. Bombay, Calcutta, Delhi, Madras: B. I. Publications.

9. Quinton, A. (1973). *Utilitarian Ethics*. London: Macmillan Publications.

10. *Bhagavad Gita* says that that one should perform one's duty, even if one can foresee the unpleasant and harmful consequences of that action. This is close to a deontological perspective. The overall justification for this position lies in the belief that Dharma is essential for general well-being of the society.

11. *https://www.poliisi.fi/poliisi/krp/home.nsf/pages/0A2FDA8FDBE427C1C2257988003B36C7?opendocument*; accessed on July 24, 2014.

12. In its resolution 55/61 of 4 December 2000, the General Assembly recognised that an effective international legal instrument against corruption, independent of the United Nations Convention against Transnational Organized Crime (resolution 55/25, annex I) was desirable and decided to establish an ad hoc committee for the negotiation of such an instrument in Vienna at the headquarters of the United Nations Office on Drugs and Crime. The convention approved by the ad hoc committee was adopted by the General Assembly by

resolution 58/4 of 31 October 2003. In accordance with article 68 (1) of resolution 58/4, the United Nations Convention against Corruption entered into force on 14 December 2005. A conference of the states parties is established to review implementation and facilitate activities required by the convention.

13. The Prevention of Corruption Act, 1988 (No. 49 of 1988) is an act of the Parliament of India enacted to combat corruption in government agencies and public sector businesses in India. The act consists of five chapters spread across 31 sections.

14. Mauro, P. (1995). "Corruption and Growth", *The Quarterly Journal of Economics* 110(3): 681–712. MIT Press.

15. Rose-Ackerman, S. (1999). *Corruption and Government: Causes, Consequences and Reform.* Cambridge University Press. p.27.

2

Corruption and Growth

All developing economies are concerned with increasing their growth rates to ensure a better quality of life for their people. However, large numbers of them are affected by problems of corruption. More than 70 per cent of the countries of the world have low values of CPI (Corruption Perceptions Index) which is used by Transparency International (TI) to measure corruption in different countries.[1] The World Bank which uses a different indicator also reports similar values for corruption. Table 2.1 indicates the picture.

Table 2.1

Countries Affected by Corruption in the Global Economy

Transparency International (2013)		*World Bank (2012)*	
CPI (Corruption Perceptions Index)	*Percentage of Countries (out of 177 Economies)*	*CCI (Control of Corruption Index)*	*Percentage of Countries (Out of 202 Economies)*
CPI <= 5.0	70.6%	CCI <= 0.0	60.4%
5.0 < CPI <= 7.0	15.3%	0.0 < CCI <= 1.25	24.8%
CPI >7.0	14.1%	CCI > 1.25	14.8%

Sources: World Bank Governance Indicators; TI.

Given the need of countries for improved quality of life and wealth for their citizens, it is important to study the effect of corruption on economic growth. There are two schools of thought in this regard. The first holds that corruption leads to slow down of economic growth and has, therefore, to be handled accordingly.[2] The second viewpoint is that corruption in many developing economies helps in continued high level of growth as it circumvents inefficient administrative procedure.[3] It is interesting to study the two alternative approaches.

According to the first school, the corrupt practice or corrupt behaviour is undesirable for growth in several ways. First, it acts as a disincentive for investment in the economy. Prospective investors are not sure about the amount of bribes they have to give to the decision-makers to enable the investments to fructify. While they can in the cost of projects include bribes which are in fact in the nature of tax for the investors, the uncertainty about its size or other details make the investments risky and hence investors may decide not to go ahead. Second, the investors are not sure of the amount of bribes which they may have to pay even after the investments have been approved at the highest level. They may have to pay bribes for getting their building plans passed or electric connections or permissions under the Labour Act or acquiring land or getting environmental clearance or any such permission required from the government. They are not sure whether they are paying too much or too little and how the system will work and what the total bribe cost will be finally. This means that they would prefer those countries where these problems are minimal. Third, during the operation of the project, the investor may have to give bribes to various officials. Since he is not sure about the amount of bribes required to be paid and how it will impact his investments, he may fear that since he would have made the investments, he would have very little choice but to sink in further money making the project less viable. This would make the proposition of investments in corrupt economies unattractive. Fourth, if the governance is weak, at every level of his operation of the industry he may have to shell out illegal money. He may be threatened with cancellation of his licence or lease for iron ore or coal mines or such other permissions like environment. New issues may be raised. It would be difficult for him to make profits after adding all costs of bribes of investing in the corrupt regime and run business efficiently. Fifth, he may not be sure what will happen in case he has won a contract after giving bribes and there is a change in the government; say the chief minister or minister concerned or senior bureaucrats or other senior officials concerned with decision-making on the project change. He may be faced with a situation where he may have to give bribe once again on the same project as the new boss may feel that he has not been adequately compensated. In all these cases, the problem arises due to bribes making the project's financial viability uncertain.

Corruption impacts investment in another manner. While with corruption contracts may be won, there is a danger that these result in poor quality of project execution. This may result in poor quality of roads, buildings which may leak and be unsuitable for residents, bridges which may get washed away, food grains or other food items like milk, medicine and such items which may be adulterated or of poor quality.[4] This will have extra maintenance cost for the economy. It will, thus, slow down construction activity as larger funds may be required for maintenance. It will also result in poor health of citizens leading to reduced human capacity for development works. It will also result in infrastructure which is perpetually under repairs and hence, slows down investments in other areas. All these are reasonable fears.

There is another worry as well when investments are being made in a corrupt economy. Increasingly, international community has got allergic to investments and contracts which have been won through illegal means. A number of countries include a clause of integrity pact in the contracts being signed. These clauses envisage that no illegal money has been paid. The UN Convention against Corruption (UNCAC) which came to force in December 2005 and to which 140 (as on June 2014) countries are signatory also envisages strict guidelines for award of contracts. The investor may be, therefore, faced with a situation where having won the contract, he is forced to sign the integrity pact. In such cases, if subsequent investigations reveal that he has won the contract by corrupt means, there is risk of cancellation and loss of money invested in the project. The recent defence contract of Agusta Westland Helicopter bought by India illustrates this point effectively. The contract signed by the company with Indian government required that there are no agents. Subsequently, it was found that there was an agent and bribes were allegedly paid. The government has cancelled the contract and encashed the bank guarantee. Having won the contract through illegal means or payment of bribe, the company has now landed in trouble.[5]

There is a contrary view as well. Many economists and sociologists argue that corruption may raise economic growth in several ways. First, it acts as an oiling machine in an otherwise corrupt regime where things may not move fast enough. By bribing officials or concerned ministers, he may get his permissions fast and his investments will, therefore, fructify early. This may lead to greater efficiency. Second, bribes may act as incentive money for officials who may work harder and thereby enable the project to run smoothly. It is like a person having an excellent rapport with all the concerned stakeholders. In this case, that rapport may be built on bribes which have been shared by all the concerned stakeholders. His permissions and files may move smoothly. As against this, in a non-corrupt regime where there is no incentive, the officials may have no interest in the project. Third, the property rights of investors in a weak legal system are at extra risk. There is poor legal protection in many such regimes. By giving bribes, he may be able to secure his property rights better. The officials who are recipients of favours may be more inclined to support him and provide protection. He may be, therefore, able to run his business smoothly. Fourth, in many regimes where large natural resources have to be explored, investments are very much localised. The corruption acts as an important tool for getting permission for development and exploration of natural resource like oil, iron ore, coal or other mineral wealth which has to be exploited. Since the choice for investment in these resources in respect of such countries is limited, the alternatives are either to forego the development of these resources and lose business opportunities or pay bribes to local officials and ministers and get permission to develop the resource. Early exploration of these resources may be in the interest of economic growth of the country which can pick up, as a result of above investments. It is well known that in many oil-rich countries, the resources are owned by nationalised companies. The governments of these countries have a strong hold over these resources. While awarding concessions, quite often the terms are notified but have some unwritten notes. Companies in order to win business may like to satisfy the requirements of various officials and ministers which are not part of the written concession agreement. These requirements could be in the form of participation in the oil field of the minister's nominee or giving bribes in some accounts or other benefits which the company can give. The choice in such heavy investments before companies is limited. In case they have to win contracts, they have to meet the illegal demands. As against that, they face domestic laws of their own countries which prohibit winning of contract through a corrupt practice. The US passed this law more than 30 years back. Recently, it has been further tightened. The UN convention on corruption has asked countries to desist from indulging in such practices. There are more than 150 state parties which are part of this convention. The choice, therefore, for companies gets limited. More than that, it is the growth of the country which gets impacted as companies win contracts to develop such resources. If there is no corruption in these states, quite often the officials and the ministers may be not very much inclined or interested to push these developments forward.[6]

Earlier Studies

The votaries of 'corruption impacting growth' have assessed the impact which corruption has on growth. The most celebrated study in this regard has been done by Paolo Mauro (1995). In his cross-country study, Mauro (1995: 681-712) has done a regression analysis with data available from 67 countries.[7] He has, for this purpose, used data from Business International (BI) on corruption for the period 1980-1983. He has evolved based on these data a bureaucratic efficiency index and classified countries on a scale of 0-10 with higher numbers indicating better efficiency of bureaucracy and lower numbers indicating lower efficiency. The index is evolved based on a selection initially of 9 criteria out of 56 'country risk' factors for which the data have been compiled by BI. Of the 9 factors, judicial system, red tape and corruption for which BI indices were available were treated as part of bureaucratic efficiency index and an average of these was taken to develop it on a scale of 0-10. Thus, countries like Australia, Belgium, Canada, Denmark, Finland, the UK, the US and similar other countries get a score of 9-10 on his index. As against this, countries like Egypt, Ghana, Indonesia, Iran, Nigeria and Pakistan get a score of 1.5–4.5. Similarly, the simple average of remaining six factors namely institutional change, social change, opposition takeover, stability of labour, relationship with neighbouring countries and terrorism have been considered as a proxy for political stability. He has also done other studies in which the average of all indices has been taken as reflecting institutional efficiency. He has considered bureaucratic efficiency as a more precise measure of corruption than the corruption index itself. In addition to above, he has also developed an index of Ethno Linguistic Fractionalisation (ELF). This index is defined as follows:

$$ELF=1-\sum_{i=1}^{i=I}\left(\frac{ni}{N}\right)^2 \qquad i=1....I$$

where n_i indicates number of people in the ith linguistic group, N is the total population and I is the number of such groups in the country. He has argued that more fractionalised a country is based on ethno-linguistic basis, larger are the chances of poorer institutional efficiency. Countries with only 1 ethnic population have a score of 0. Countries up to a high number of 100 such groups were assessed by him. He argued that there is a negative and significant correlation between institutional efficiency and ELF. He has computed that ELF index has a simple correlation coefficient (r) of -0.38 with the Institutional Index, -0.41 with the Political Stability Index, -0.28 with Bureaucratic Efficiency Index and -0.31 with Corruption Index.

Based on the above development of indices, he regressed corruption against investment as a percentage of GDP (gross domestic product), and per capita GDP growth for the period of 1960-1985. The results of regression concluded that during 1960-1985, one standard deviation improvement in the bureaucratic efficiency index (BI) is associated with an increase in investment rate by 4.75 per cent of GDP. Subsequently, he argued that per capita GDP growth is significantly associated with bureaucratic efficiency. He also estimated that one standard deviation improvement in corruption index (it is one of the components of BI) is associated with an increase in investment rate by 2.9 per cent of GDP. The results showed that corruption index association with investment rate of GDP is not robust. This implies that overall efficiencies of governance including judicial processes and bureaucracy and red tape, which involve efficiencies of implementations and approvals, are major determinants of growth process. By itself, corruption does not have a strong relationship with growth.

The analysis by Mauro mentioned above has been given in some details to explain the perspective and methodology. Mauro has done the pioneering work in studying various aspects of corruption, investment and growth in cross-country framework. It is, however, clear that the parameters used by him do not fully explain either per capita growth or investment. Even though, he used several independent explanatory variables including GDP in 1960 (his study covers the period 1960-1985), secondary education, population growth, primary education, government expenditure, revolutions and coups, assassination and purchasing price power parity value for investment deflators and dummies for Latin America and Africa, the explanation of growth and corruption relationship was not very clear.[8]

The study also assumes that bureaucratic efficiency is a better indicator of corruption index. This has created a problem of comparison in different studies since the definition of corruption is not comparable. Another important issue is the period covered for the study by him. After 1980, a number of Asian economies have moved rapidly and undertaken economic and institutional reforms and opened their economies to private investment. Countries like Singapore, Japan, Malaysia and China have been undertaking series of reforms during this period. There is a need to look at longer periods. It is particularly important since several new data sources are now available measuring corruption.

As mentioned earlier, the school of thought on corruption adversely impacting growth was also supported by many studies. Broadly, they have held the view that corruption had a negative impact on investment. The argument in many of these studies was that corrupt officials create delays and barriers that otherwise do not exist. These are restrictions on trade which are rent seeking.[9] It is argued that "political corruption or grand corruption distorts the entire decision making process connected with public investments. The degree of distortion is higher with weak auditing institutions."[10] They hold that higher corruption has association with higher public investment which gives ample opportunities to politicians to indulge in corrupt practices and make money. It results in lower government revenues, lower expenditure on O&M (operations & maintenance) of assets and this is connected with poor quality of infrastructure. It is argued that high public investment along with high corruption leads to lower productivity. The study indicates five channels through which corruption lowers growth.

In a cross-country analysis for the period 1975-2001, a study by Dreher and Herzfeld (2005), estimates effect of corruption on economic growth and per capita GDP. It concludes that increase in corruption by one index point reduces GDP growth by 0.13 per cent and per capita GDP by $ 425. It also estimates similar average yearly reduction in per capita GDP and GDP growth due to above average level of corruption. The average reduction in growth rate projected by their methodology is much lower than other estimates. While recognising this, the authors offer no possible explanation.[11] The losses due to corruption are especially high in countries from African economy and been increasing in transition economies since 1980. Guinea-Bissau was the world's most corrupt country in 1991-1997 with a loss of 70 per cent of its potential GDP. These estimates decline to 27 per cent (1998–2002) if a different set of explanatory variables was used.[12]

The other school with a more understanding stance on corruption has several followers but there is a wide variety in their analysis. Some argue that after controlling for investments, corruption lowered growth, while others find that there is no statistically significant direct relationship once other factors are controlled.[13] There are, however, indirect effects as corruption effects investment, schooling, trade policies and political stability. Some studies have found a significant positive relationship between GDP per capita growth and increased corruption.[14] Analysing East Asian countries, some studies found significant positive impact of increased corruption on growth, while in other developing countries, it was found to be negative.[15] There are also studies which say that "to the extent we can measure corruption in a cross-country setting, it does not affect growth."[16]

Houston (2007) emphasises that institutional protection of property is deficient in a number of countries which are poor. Measures on reducing corruption or fighting against corruption in these countries result in policies opposing increase in domestic investment. It damages the effort of people who "drive to build a market economy using the resources at hand." He analyses the components of corruption, and also identifies expansionary effect of corruption and restrictive effect of corruption. Following other works he divides corrupt action into two categories: economically restrictive and economically expansionary. In expanding activity, he gives an example of citizens bribing officials to evade bad laws. He also talks of indirect tax of corruption which might restrict the gain of an expansionary growth. He then computes losses from corruption as against gains from corruption in 119 countries and finds that for 12 countries, it gives positive benefits.[17]

We have also looked at several other recent works which argue that: "Corruption can have a positive effect on growth, most likely by allowing people to circumvent inefficient policies. By breaking down the economic freedom index into each of its five areas, it is found that corruption is only significantly growth enhancing when countries have low level of freedom in the area of government size, freedom of trade internationally, regulation of credit, labor and business. When economic freedom in the area of government size and regulations improved, the benefits of corruption for growth significantly declined and eventually turned negative." It was also found that instead of political freedom, it was ultimately the economic freedom of institutions and policies which needed to be addressed.[18]

Bardhan (1997) has not undertaken any separate cross-country regression analysis but considered the impact of corruption on efficiency of investment and the growth process. He mentions that in the US and European history during the 18th century and later, there was a great deal of corruption in giving concessions, licences, mining loans and other benefits given by the state. This led to development of a class of entrepreneurs. Historically, while corruption may have played an important role in many developing countries, in modern society it is not likely to have good net effect. He observes that corruption tends to feed on itself and it is impossible to confine and restrict its effects to any specific area. Commenting on cross-sectional studies, he makes a point that policy issues on corruption cannot be discussed without considering the state which implements these policies. He specifically mentions problems with data sets which are collected by persons who have no local knowledge or experience and may pay higher bribes and thus give data not consistent with ground realities.[19]

There are a number of other studies which have through cross-sectional analysis computed impact of corruption on growth. While increase in corruption by one index point reduces growth by 0.13 per cent according to Dreher and Herzfeld (2005), similar level of increase in corruption index reduces growth by 0.5 per cent (Aizenman and Glick, 2003) and 0.39-0.41 per cent (Gyimah-Brempong, 2002). Mauro (1995) has in his work estimated that investment to GDP increases by 2.9 per cent by one standard deviation increase in corruption index. Using the standard deviation computed by him, it works out to 1.17 per cent increase for one index value increase in corruption. This could result in increased GDP growth of 0.23 per cent to 0.29 per cent assuming capital output ratio of 4 to 5. The average capital output ratio during 1985 was 3.6. All these estimates indicate that reduced corruption of one index value increases GDP growth by 0.13 to 0.50 per cent per annum. The lowest estimate is of Dreher and Herzfeld (2005), who recognise this fact but do not offer any explanation for their estimate being so widely different from other authors.[20]

Our Approach

We have analysed the impact of corruption on growth for the period 1996-2012. Apart from studies mentioned earlier, there is also a general perception that corruption slows growth. A lot of it is influenced by moral standpoint and debates in the civil society universe and in international fora. Studies as mentioned above for the period 1960-1985 by Mauro and a number of other economists and sociologists give a mixed picture. Many of these studies were, however, confined to a limited number of countries, and pertained to a period when many of the Asian economies had not stepped up growth. Specially, this was prior to acceleration of the growth process in India and China. Since then data have become available from TI on corruption index for a much larger number of countries.[21] Also, the World Bank has prepared governance index which includes corruption as one of the factors and this index is prepared separately. The sources of the World Bank and the TI index are quite broad based as mentioned earlier, as far as perception-based corruption data are concerned. We use these data sources. We study economic growth–corruption relationship in three parts.

In part I, we consider investment/GDP and corruption relationship for 147 countries for the period 1996-2012. We also identify several other independent variables apart from corruption, and take average values for all variables during this period and treat investment/GDP as a dependent variable.

In part II, we consider GDP growth and corruption relationship. We use several independent variables and take average values over the period 1996-2012. We treat GDP growth as a dependent variable. We also consider the impact of corruption on some of the independent variables and account for this finally in estimating the total impact of corruption on economic growth. We also consider this relationship in different groups of countries. For this purpose, we use World Bank classification of dividing global economies into low income, lower middle income, upper middle income and high income groups. We consider as to how the corruption-GDP growth relationship changes in each of these groups.

In part III, we consider per capita income and corruption relationship in the same period 1996-2012. We take averages of all the variables for this period. We consider the same independent variables for working out the relationship as used for GDP growth. We treat per capita income as a dependent variable and others including corruption as independent variables. Like earlier analysis, we take averages during the period 1996-2012 for all variables to study the relationship. We again identify independent variables impacted by corruption and account for this in computing the total impact of corruption on per capita GDP. We also consider different groups of countries on the same classification as done for studying GDP growth-corruption relationship. We then identify how this relationship changes in different income groups. We also identify the change in different income groups due to indirect impact of corruption on some independent variables.

Part I

In this part, we study the relationship between investment/GDP and corruption index for the period 1996–2012. We treat corruption as an independent variable and investment/GDP as a dependent variable. In Table 2.2, our results are compared with a similar study done by Mauro.

Table 2.2

Investment/GDP Dependence on Corruption

Period	*1980-1985**	*1960-1985**	*1996-2012***
Constant	0.125 (6.63)	0.086 (4.14)	23.30 (12.09)
Corruption Index	0.0117 (4.41)	0.018 (6.43)	-0.072 (-0.2034)
Number of Countries	67	58	153
R^2	0.18	0.40	0.000275

Source: World Bank Governance Indicators, 2012; *: Mauro (1995); **: Our Results.

Table 2.2 indicates that results of the two studies are quite different. Our study is for 153 countries unlike Mauro which was limited to about 60 countries and for a different time period. While Mauro finds a strong relationship between investment/GDP and corruption with increase in corruption leading to reduction in investment/GDP, we find no relationship in these two variables. The investment to GDP ratio amongst different countries seems to lack any association with corruption. There are several reasons for this difference. During 1960-1985 period, investors had a wide choice. The investment was put in countries with low level of corruption. The Asian economies and also the African economies had not emerged then and had poor infrastructure discouraging any investment. As the economies developed potential for growth, in spite of heavy corruption prevalent in many countries, investment was made. In several of these, there were large oil reserves. The investments were, therefore, made ignoring high corruption levels and utilising the potential for profits which the investments required. The emergence of India, China, Malaysia, Thailand and Indonesia as high growth potential countries also led to break down of this relationship. The change of global environment is thus evident in the two periods 1960-1985 and 1996-2012.

Table 2.3

Secular Trend of Exports and Investment of Developing and Developed Economies

	1980-1985	*1996-2012*
Developing Economies Export (% of World total)	27	37
Developed Economies Export (% of World total)	70	61
Developed Economies (Investment/GDP) (%)	25	23
Developing Economies (Investment/GDP) (%)	24	24.1

Note: Investment includes both public and private investment; IMF divides world economies into developed, developing and emerging market economies. Apart from the investment details mentioned for developed and developing groups of economies, rest of the world investment goes to emerging market economies.

Source: UNCTAD; IMF, *World Economic Outlook,* April 2014.

The revolution of rising expectation led to countries wanting a better quality of life. National governments responded to these aspirations and brought about changes in domestic policies. It led to increase in investment/GDP ratio. As mentioned above, the reforms in China started in late 1970s with India following suit with major reforms in early 1990s. Other nations similarly brought about changes in their economies. Because of corruption, the project cost increased. However, the developing countries had lower labour costs. The economies produced goods for the domestic market at a competitive price. They also exported these to other countries. The share of global exports went up resulting in increased reserves (Table 2.3). Therefore in spite of high level of corruption, the last two decades saw increased investment/GDP in several of these economies. The impact of corruption hence was sharply reduced. The investments in these economies were governed more by domestic economic policies, political stability and desire to step up growth, as well as development of infrastructure. People were willing to make investments after taking into account costs of corruption in their project cost and circumventing inefficiencies by giving bribes. Thus, the two periods are so widely different that the same methodology gives completely different results.

Table 2.3 clearly indicates that both investments and exports in the developing economies increased as compared to Organisation for Economic Co-operation and Development (OECD) countries.

This change was manifest in a number of large Asian and African economies. The breakdown of relationship with corruption in a number of countries reflected the above position.

However, the investment/GDP ratio which is the vehicle for growth does get impacted when we consider economies with different features and relation with corruption at different levels of education, political stability, voice and accountability, per capita GDP, inflation and such other factors. As these variables differ in different countries, the impact of corruption becomes more manifest in some of these groups. While at a global level, the investment/GDP relationship with corruption during 1996-2012 is extremely weak, in different groups of countries including African, Asian economies, OECD and other groups, the impact of corruption is more manifest (Annexure Table A-2.1). The regression analysis indicates several features:

First, all individual groups including Asian, African, OECD and others had a strong association of corruption with investment/GDP during above period.

Second, in African economies, high corruption was associated with high investment/GDP. In other groups, increased corruption adversely affected investment/GDP. While in OECD countries corruption was not an issue, in Asian economies lower corruption was associated with higher investment/GDP. This is significant. It possibly represents the opportunities for investors in these countries as the economies had opened up. It is also indicative of the fact that in this group, countries where corruption levels were high, investments did not take place and growth was lower.

Third, political stability and governance had very large positive impact on investment in Africa. It was less so in other groups.

Part II

In this part of our analysis, we consider several independent variables which affect GDP growth and explain inter-country variation in these. We select total investment/GDP ratio, GDP per capita in 1996, corruption, political stability, voice and accountability, secondary education and government expenditure to GDP as independent variables. We treat GDP growth as a dependent variable.

We take averages for both dependent and independent variables for the period 1996-2012. Data for 141 countries are taken for analysis. Let us briefly mention the rationale for selecting various independent variables.

Investment/GDP is a key factor determining growth and we use this. High government expenditure can crowd out private borrowing opportunities if government revenues are not buoyant. In countries with high corruption, there is a lot of leakage and theft. Government tax realisation hence goes down. In such countries, if government wishes to increase expenditure, it does so by borrowing from the market adversely affecting private investment. Productivity of government expenditure is comparatively low as against private investments. We, therefore, use government expenditure/GDP as an independent variable.

Inflation is a key factor in determining savings, investment and growth. Corrupt regimes often have high inflation due to theft of available resources and artificial shortages caused by appropriation of public welfare goods by a coterie. In India, this is seen in distribution of food grains and sugar under PDS (public distribution system). Government servants, politicians and the fair price shop owners continue to corner subsidised goods and sell them at high prices. A number of times, onion have disappeared from the market due to hoarding by middlemen. All these cases of corruption result in food inflation and affect growth. A moderate level of inflation supports growth. We account for this by taking per capita income in 1996 and GDP growth on $2,005 constant level.

Human resource development is another factor affecting growth. We feel skill development or opportunities which arise from secondary education can help reduce corruption. Secondary school education is important for attaining skills. It is of course possible to do this with primary education also; but in most of the nations of global community, we have reached very high level of primary education. Selecting this variable would not distinguish differences in various countries, which is to be explained in a cross-country analysis. We have, hence, chosen secondary school education as an explanatory variable. This has been done by several other studies earlier too.[22]

We have also considered the need for taking political stability as a variable. Global experience shows that in many countries of Africa, Asia and Latin America, this is an important factor. The democracy in many of these countries is yet to take full root. The institutions for development and growth of the economy depend a lot on political stability of the country. This instability comes from various factors. In the oil rich countries of the Middle East namely Iraq, Iran, South Arabia, Qatar and Libya and the African oil rich countries like Nigeria and Angola, the stability of regimes is an important factor for investments and production. Ongoing war in Iraq is hardly conducive to economic growth of the region. In several Latin American countries like Venezuela, Columbia, Mexico and Brazil, this is again an important factor. Political regime stability is crucial for effective implementation of regulatory policies and efficiency of investments. We have, therefore, considered this also as an independent variable.

Voice and accountability is another important factor which we have considered for its impact on growth. The efficiency of public investment is important for growth. Large private investment can come if government is considered accountable for its policies. It is true that there can be higher growth rates in economies which are autocratic and not accountable to its people. South Korea, Malaysia and Singapore are such examples. But as an overall policy regime, countries which are answerable to their people will generally function in a democratic manner. Investors are liable to raise their voice against problems. Their voices can also be carried by other players. We have, therefore, considered this as a variable which impacts growth.

The initial stage of economic development of a country invariably affects its potential for growth. Per capita income is a good indicator for this. In line with other studies done, we have used this, too, as an explanatory variable. We have, in addition to above, used corruption as an independent variable. We consider all these variables including corruption to understand cross-country GDP growth variation. We do a similar exercise with different income groups. The results of regression analysis (Annexure Tables A-2.2 and A-2.3) show a good explanatory capability of independent variables. It indicates several features as mentioned below.

First, the regression analysis indicates that the GDP growth may increase by 0.37 per cent, if an increase of one index value in corruption takes place or corruption reduces. We do a two-stage analysis to account for impact of corruption on other independent variables. We have separately assessed this dependence of each independent variable through regression analysis. Those coefficients along with the direction of impact (whether +ve or -ve) are then applied to the equation to find out total impact. We find that the increase in GDP growth is 0.40 per cent by reduced corruption of one index point. These results are quite in line with others.[23]

Second, the impact of reduced corruption in different income groups is not uniform. Lower corruption in low income countries has a large impact on growth. The potential for growth is very high in low income countries. The investment required for increasing growth is small and there are large inefficiencies in use of resources. A small effort gives good result. As incomes rise, larger investments are required and technology plays a bigger part. Growth needs more comprehensive policy intervention. In low income group, one index value reduced corruption lowers growth by 0.49 per cent. The impact is higher in lower middle income group of countries. In these economies, lower corruption of one index value reduces growth by 0.73 per cent. The impact reduces thereafter with lower one index corruption being associated with 0.30 per cent reduced growth in upper middle income group of countries and 0.09 per cent reduction in high income countries. It clearly brings out that corruption is causing maximum damage to growth efforts in lower middle income group of countries. India falls in this group.

Third, GDP growth has positive relation with investment/GDP and political stability. With increase in their values, GDP growth is expected to be positive. Of these, the strongest relationship is with investment/GDP for which we have taken average value over the study period. An increase of 1.0 per cent in this ratio increases growth by 0.16 per cent. This is clearly not very high investment efficiency but increases with other variables joining it. The political stability is helpful for growth. Increase in its index value by 1.0, increases growth by 0.13 per cent. Voice and accountability, too, has a positive impact.

This impact of these institutions is strongest in low income economies with per capita income of less than $1,035. In other income groups, it is almost insignificant. Nearly 85 per cent of these are economies from the African continent. An improved governance of political institutions has a very large impact on economic growth. The sensitivity to good governance is clearly very high in low income nations.

Fourth, rates of growth in high per capita countries are lower than others. As per capita incomes increase, rates of growth get affected adversely. This is reflective of a strong growth potential in many developing economies. This is borne out by our experience during this period. The average GDP growth of developing economies during 1996-2012 was 4.4 per cent as against 2.4 per cent of OECD nations.[24] A weak negative correlation with government expenditure reflects its low efficiency. Faster growth is supported by larger private investment, smaller public investment and also government expenditure.

Fifth, secondary school education is expected to fuel growth with availability of larger young population with potential for skills. The results show otherwise. An increase in secondary school education is likely to reduce growth, though by a very small measure. Two explanations are possible. In an ageing society, secondary school employment may go down as there is need for more workers. An alternative explanation is that increased share of such boys and girls which are in the 14-20 age group reduces availability of employed workers leading to reduced employment and income in developing economies. Both explanations appear feasible and probable.

Part III

We consider in this part results of the regression analysis of per capita income with corruption. The per capita income is treated as a dependent variable. The regression analysis is done for 147 countries. The factors which impact per capita income are treated as independent variables. We take the same independent variables for this analysis as used above for GDP growth. We do the regression analysis for all economies together and also for different income groups as identified earlier. We take average for each variable for the period 1996-2012 for each country. We find that the explanatory variables provide a very good explanation of variations in per capita income of different countries (Annexure Tables A-2.4 and A-2.5) during this period of all economies taken together and in each income group. Some important features of the analysis are mentioned below.

First, the analysis shows that with an increase in index of corruption by one unit, the per capita income during 1996-2012 could go up by $304.7. We also estimate the indirect impact of corruption on other variables to work out its total impact. For this, we consider separately impact of corruption on each independent variable. The results show a strong relation of corruption with two specific parameters: political stability and voice and accountability. Both these impact ability of the governance system to be able to perform and be accountable for it. Lower corruption by one index value results in increased income of $108.2 of per capita GDP due to better political stability, and it leads to $39.2 increased income in voice and accountability segment. The total indirect impact of increase of one unit of corruption index is increase in per capita income by $147.4. The total impact is about $450 after accounting for other impacts. It is 4.5 per cent of the average of per capita world GDP during this period.

Second, in different income groups, lower corruption by one index value would have large impact on low income economies. In the four income groups referred earlier, lower corruption of one index value would increase per capita income in low income group by $281 and in the lower middle income group by $329. Its impact starts declining thereafter. In upper middle income group, its impact is $287 and in high income group, it is only $65 for similar level of lower corruption.

Third, political stability, voice and accountability and investment/ GDP show a positive relation with per capita income. This indicates that in more stable regimes with stronger accountability, per capita incomes are higher. Also, higher investment/GDP results in higher per capita incomes. This is quite in accordance with expected association of these variables with per capita income.

Fourth, the secondary school enrolment again shows a negative coefficient for all economies taken together. This signifies that with increase in secondary school education, per capita income comes down especially in high income countries. This, as mentioned earlier, is partly explained by reduced employment opportunities for this age groups leading to lower employment. In low income nations, there is a desire to improve education levels. In these economies, enrolment is higher with increasing incomes as confirmed by regression results.

Fifth, government expenditure is high in countries with higher per capita income. As incomes go up, tax revenues are generally higher. Governments tend to spend more on health, social security, education and similar other factors. This is much more pronounced in high income and upper middle income countries. These countries are able to provide larger social benefits which the low income or lower middle income countries are not able to. Because of this, the government expenditure shows a positive coefficient for the higher income group of countries. For low income countries, government expenditure depends upon efficiency of tax realisation and aid funds. Higher per capita incomes do not necessarily imply larger revenues. They may show lower government expenditure, which enables higher private borrowing and investments.

Lastly, we also consider the impact of corruption on per capita GDP in some countries assuming that countries which are below average in corruption index (higher corruption) are able to reach corruption levels to the world average or to the average corruption levels in Scandinavian countries. (Annexure Tables A-2.6 and A-2.7). Since in case of many countries this involves large improvement in levels of corruption which they may not be able to achieve, we also indicate the impact of one index value increase on growth. We find that if countries are able to address problem of corruption both growth rates and per capita incomes can go up. If India had been able to reduce corruption to the level of Scandinavian countries in 1996 and continued at that level, other things being equal, our average of per capita incomes for 1996-2012 would be three times or $2,928 at 2005 constant US$ instead of $746. Also GDP growth would be higher in the entire period by 1.8 per cent per annum.

Conclusion

The study of relationship of GDP growth and per capita income in the cross-country regression analysis brings out several important results. These can be used as major determinant of public policy on reducing corruption and stepping up growth in different countries. It is clear that with increased level of corruption by one index value, the GDP growth goes down by around 0.4 per cent per annum and per capita incomes are lost to the extent of $450. Both of these are very significant impacts. The analysis even within the various income groups indicates the highest potential growth in low middle income countries. Lower corruption has an impact which is twice that of any other group for them. If they are able to reduce corruption by four index points, it can give them extra growth of about 2 per cent per annum. This growth will come out of increased efficiency of investments and possibly some new investments. The loss of growth and income is quite large in the context of these economies.

Notes and References

1. TI is a non-governmental organisation that monitors and publicises corporate and political corruption in international development. Originally founded in Germany in May 1993 as a not-for-profit organisation, TI is now an international non-governmental organisation. It publishes an annual *Global Corruption Barometer* and *Corruption Perceptions Index*, a comparative listing of corruption worldwide. The headquarters are located in Berlin, Germany.
2. Myrdal, Gunnar (1970). "Corruption as a Hindrance to Modernization in South Asia", in Arnold J. Heidenheimer (ed.), Political Corruption: Reading in Comparative Analysis. New York: Holt, Rinehart & Winston. p.230; See also, Leff, Nathaniel H. (1964). "'Economic Development through Bureaucratic Corruption", *The American Behavioral Scientist* 8(2): 8-14, November.
3. Huntington, Samuel P. (1968). *Political Order in Changing Societies*. New Haven: Yale University Press.
4. Tanzi, V. and Hamid R. Davoodi (2000). "Corruption, Growth, and Public Finances", *IMF Working Paper* WP/00/182.
5. In early 2013, an Indian parliamentary investigation began into allegations of bribery and corruption involving several senior officials and helicopter manufacturer Agusta Westland surrounding the purchase of a new fleet of helicopters. Several Indian politicians and military officials have been accused of accepting bribes from Agusta Westland in order to win the ₹ 36 billion (US$ 600 million) Indian contract for the supply of 12 Agusta Westland AW 101 helicopters; these helicopters are intended to perform VVIP duties for the President of India and other important state officials.
6. Heckelman, Jac C. and Benjamin Powell (2010). "Corruption and the Institutional Environment for Growth", *Comparative Economic Studies* 52(3): 351-78, September. Palgrave Macmillan.
7. Regression analysis involves taking a dependent variable and studying its relationship with one or more independent variables. The study aims to see whether independent variable explains the behaviour or dependent variable. A good example is prices. If this is treated as

dependent variable, inflation can be considered independent variable. Higher the inflation, higher is the price increases due to inflation. See also: Mauro, P. (1995). "Corruption and Growth", *The Quarterly Journal of Economics* 110(3): 681–712. MIT Press.

8. R^2 value is a regression analysis that indicates the extent to which the movement of dependent variable is explained by explanatory independent variable. A value of 1 indicates perfect association and 0 indicates no association. In Mauro studies, the R^2 values vary between 0.44 and 0.66 for various scenarios.
9. Shleifer, A. and R.W. Vishny (1993). "Corruption", *Quarterly Journal of Economics* 108 (3): 599-617; See also: Myrdal, Gunnar (1968). Asian Drama: An Inquiry into the Poverty of Nations. 3 Vols. Allen Lane: The Penguin Press; Wei, S.–J. (2000). "How Taxing is Corruption on International Investors", *Review of Economics and Statistics* LXXXII(1): 1-11.
10. Tanzi, Vito and Hamid R. Davoodi (1997). "Corruption, Public Investment, and Growth", *IMF Working Paper*, October, pp.1-23. Available at SSRN: *http://ssrn.com/abstract=882701*
11. They have also considered six transmission channels through which corruption impact growth in these countries namely, inflation, aid, school enrolment, life expectancy, government expenditure as a percentage of GDP, and investment as a percentage of GDP. See also: Dreher, Axel and Thomas Herzfeld (2005). "The Economic Costs of Corruption: A Survey and New Evidence", *Public Economics* 0506001. EconWPA. Available at *SSRN: http://ssrn.com/abstract=734184 or http://dx.doi.org/10.2139/ssrn.734184*
12. Dreher, A., C. Kotsogiannis and S. McCorriston (2007). "Corruption around the World: Evidence from a Structural Model", *Journal of Comparative Economics* 35: 443-66.
13. Mo, Pak Hung (2000). "Income Inequality and Economic Growth", *Kyklos* 53(3): 293–316; See also: Pellegrini L. and R. Gerlagh (2004). "Corruption's Effect on Growth and its Transmission Channels", *Kyklos* 57(3): 429-56.
14. Perotti, Roberto (1994). "Income Distribution and Investment", European Econ. Rev. 38(3): 827–35.
15. Rock, M.T. and H. Bonnett (2004). "The Comparative Politics of Corruption: Accounting for the East Asian Paradox in Empirical Studies of Corruption, Growth and Investment", *World Development* 32(6): 999-1017.
16. Svensson J. (2005). "Eight Questions About Corruption", *Journal of Economic Perspectives* 19(3): 19-42.
17. Houstan, Douglas A. (2007). "Can Corruption Ever Improve an Economy?", *Cato Journal* 27(3): 325-42.
18. Heckelman, Jac C. and Benjamin Powell (2008). "Corruption and the Institutional Environment for Growth"', *Research Working Paper* 2008-6. Suffolk University.
19. Bardhan, P. (1997). "Corruption and Development: A Review of Issues", *Journal of Economic Literature* 35(3): 1320-46, September. American Economic Association.
20. Gyimah-Brempong, K. (2002). "Corruption, Economic Growth, and Income Inequality in Africa", *Economics of Governance* 3: 183–209; See also: Aizenman, J. and R. Glick (2003). "Military Expenditure, Threats, and Growth", *NBER Working Papers* 9618. National Bureau of Economic Research Inc; Mauro, P. (1995). "Corruption and Growth", *The Quarterly Journal of Economics* 110(3): 681–712. MIT Press.
21. Based on a long-standing research programme of the World Bank, the Worldwide Governance Indicators capture six key dimensions of governance (voice and accountability, political stability and lack of violence, government effectiveness, regulatory quality, rule of law and control of corruption) between 1996 and present. They measure the quality of governance

in over 200 countries, based on close to 40 data sources produced by over 30 organisations worldwide and are updated annually since 2002.

22. Mauro, P. (1995). "Corruption and Growth", *The Quarterly Journal of Economics* 110(3): 681–712. MIT Press. See also: Dreher, Axel and Thomas Herzfeld (2005). "The Economic Costs of Corruption: A Survey and New Evidence", *Public Economics* 0506001. EconWPA. Available at *SSRN: http://ssrn.com/abstract=734184 or http://dx.doi.org/10.2139/ssrn.734184*
23. Dreher, Axel and Thomas Herzfeld (2005). "The Economic Costs of Corruption: A Survey and New Evidence", *Public Economics* 0506001. EconWPA. Available at *SSRN: http://ssrn.com/abstract=734184 or http://dx.doi.org/10.2139/ssrn.734184*; See also note no. 19.
24. World Bank (2012). *World Bank Development Indicators.* available at: *http://data.worldbank.org/data-catalog/world-development-indicators.*

Annexure Table A-2.1

Investment/GDP Average (1996-2012) Regression
(Investment/GDP is the dependent variable)

Independent Variable (s)	*All Economies Together*	*African Economies*	*Asian Economies*	*OECD Economies*	*Rest of the Economies*
Constant	25.57 (6.10)	43.49 (5.052)	3.21 (0.344)	22.70 (2.245)	14.11 (3.73)
GDP Per Capita (Constant 2005 US$) in '000	0.0281 (0.29)	2.96 (3.49)	-0.648 (-2.91)	-0.767 (-1.595)	-0.118 (-1.275)
Foreign Exchange Reserve/GDP	8.97 (1.57)	15.72 (1.084)	8.65 (0.8593)	15.698 (2.168)	6.96 (1.298)
CPI, Inflation (%)	-0.033 (-0.1739)	-0.062 (-1.655)	0.3555 (0.8211)	-0.151 (-1.14)	0.043 (0.7607)
Secondary School Education (%)	0.0121 (0.3395)	-0.1482 (-1.44)	0.01635 (0.222)	0.1300 (2.285)	0.0699 (2.056)
Government Expenditure/ GDP	-0.1425 (-0.8502)	0.2397 (0.5429)	-0.4281 (-1.184)	-0.272 (-1.95)	0.201 (0.9788)
Corruption Index (0-10) Average (1996-2012)	-0.6731 (-0.239)	-0.90 (-1.719)	0.839 (2.341)	0.114 (1.323)	0.455 (0.375)
Political Stability (0-10) Average (1996-2012)	0.8803 (0.551)	1.24 (1.897)	0.101 (0.133)	0.128 (1.243)	0.511 (0.5771)
Governance Index (0-10) Average (1996-2012)	1.3035 (1.597)	1.25 (1.234)	0.217 (0.9704)	0.085 (0.3127)	0.437 (0.495)
Number of Countries	147	40	28	31	47
R^2	0.264	0.583	0.541	0.570	0.257

Note: Governance index is estimated by computing arithmetic average of indices of government effectiveness, voice and accountability, rule of law, and regulatory quality. The t values are in brackets.

Annexure Table A-2.2

GDP Growth (%) Average (1996-2012) Regression (All Economies Together)

Independent Variable(s)	*Dependent Variable is GDP Growth (%) Average (1996-2012)*							
Constant	2.852 (1.382)	2.683 (1.77)	2.493 (3.391)	2.315 (3.454)	2.301 (4.066)	2.300 (4.35)	2.239 (5.096)	2.113 (4.346)
Total Investment/ GDP (1996-2012) Average (%)	0.171 (10.68)	0.166 (11.26)	0.166 (11.55)	0.168 (11.41)	0.159 (10.61)	0.162 (10.96)	0.162 (11.25)	0.1625 (11.2)
GDP Per Capita (1996) in '000		-.053 (-4.73)	-.0605 (-.307)	-.0621 (-.376)	-.0628 (-.631)	-.00862 (-.448)	-.0139 (-.726)	-.0135 (-0.710)
Corruption Index (0-10) (1996-2012) Average			0.348 (2.86)	0.350 (1.75)	0.355 (1.78)	.0.358 (1.84)	0.361 (1.706)	0.365 (1.765)
Political Stability Index (0-10) (1996-2012) Average				0.105 (.836)	0.1162 (1.126)	0.1287 (1.22)	0.1318 (1.258)	0.132 (1.235)
Voice and Accountability Index (0-10) (1996-2012) Average					.3364 (2.41)	.2614 (1.85)	0.248 (1.18)	0.158 (1.834)
Secondary Education (%)						-.01298 (-2.282)	-.0112 (-2.01)	-.0077 (-1.26)
Government Expenditure/GDP (1996-2012) (%)							-.077 (-2.80)	-.0772 (-2.54)
Number of countries	141	141	141	141	141	141	141	141
R^2	0.491	0.501	0.508	0.517	0.526	0.584	0.612	0.662

Note: Regression Table A-2.2 has no column heads as it is a waterfall representation with each successive column indicating results of regression analysis after an additional independent variable mentioned in the corresponding row is considered.

Source: GDP Growth (%) from the World Bank; Investment/GDP ratio (%) involves both public and private investments; it is from IMF; Government Expenditure/GDP ratio (%) is from World Bank; Political Instability Index is from World Bank, and is on a scale of 0-10 (higher the index, lower the political instability).

Annexure Table A-2.3

GDP Growth (%) Average (1996-2012) Regression of Various Groups of Economies

	Dependent Variable is GDP Growth(%) Average (1996-2012)				
Independent Variable(s)	*Low Income*	*Lower Middle Income*	*Upper Middle Income*	*High Income*	*All Economies*
Constant	5.773 (2.342)	1.592 (1.25)	3.370 (1.46)	0.9837 (0.510)	3.113 (4.346)
Total Investment/ GDP (1996-2012) Average (%)	0.057 (0.504)	0.109 (3.35)	0.155 (2.41)	0.188 (10.69)	0.1625 (11.2)
GDP, Per Capita (1996) in '000 Average (1996-2012)	-8.00 (-2.05)	-1.201 (-2.97)	-.4900 (-3.29)	-.00627 (-0.35)	-.0135 (-0.71)
Corruption Index (0-10) Average (1996-2012)	0.487 (1.58)	0.731 (2.393)	0.296 (1.68)	0.0913 (0.395)	0.365 (1.765)
Political Instability (0-10) Average (1996-2012)	0.531 (1.33)	0.064 (0.400)	0.114 (1.15)	0.091 (0.58)	0.132 (1.235)
Voice and Accountability 0-10 Average (1996-2012)	0.182 (1.96)	0.006 (0.034)	0.092 (0.145)	-0.015 (-1.63)	0.158 (1.834)
Secondary Education (%) Average (1996-2012) (%)	-.009 (-.342)	0.0062 (0.803)	-.0089 (-.612)	0.0089 (0.435)	-.011 (-2.04)
Government Expenditure/GDP Average (1996-2012) (%)	-.089 (-1.01)	-0.132 (-3.94)	-.0190 (-.219)	-0.0434 (-0.84)	-.0772 (-2.77)
Number of countries	24	32	27	39	122
R^2	0.53	0.768	0.563	0.927	0.653

Note: Secondary Education Enrolment (%) represents the number of students enrolled in secondary education in percentage to the number of students in that official age group. For some of countries, this value is higher than 100 per cent, which means that some of the students enrolled in the secondary education are from outside the officially accepted age group. The t values are in brackets.

Source: GDP Growth (%) from the World Bank; investment/GDP ratio (%) involves both public and private investments; it is from IMF. Government Expenditure/GDP ratio (%) is from World Bank; Political Instability Index is from World Bank, and is on a scale of 0-10 (higher the index, lower the political instability). Corruption Index is from World Bank, and is on a scale of 0-10 (higher the index, lower the corruption). Voice and Accountability Index is from World Bank, and is on a scale of 0-10 (higher the index, higher the freedom of expression). GDP, per capita is at constant 2005 $ and has been taken from the *World Bank Development Indicators, 2012.*

Annexure Table A-2.4

GDP Per Capita Average (1996-2012) Regression (All Economies Together)

	Dependent Variable GDP Per Capita Average (1996-2012)							
Constant	-20674 (-11.52)	-20139 (-10.3)	-19476 (-9.584)	-20106 (-9.73)	-18939 (-7.929)	-19759 (-8.07)	-19706 (-6.44)	-3775.4 (-4.73)
Corruption Index (1996-2012) Average 0-10 Scale	6094.8 (18.29)	6390.4 (11.84)	6867.32 (10.18)	6573.81 (9.40)	6702.4 (9.41)	6790.0 (9.54)	6788.7 (9.44)	304.7 (0.247)
Political Stability Index (1996-2012) Average 0-10 Scale		-419.8 (-0.697)	-278.43 (-0.45)	-276.87 (-0.453)	-238.17 (-0.389)	-171.4 (-1.37)	-166.4 (-0.262)	153.19 (1.013)
Voice and Accountability Index (1996-2012) Average 0-10 Scale			-750.14 (-1.17)	-933.55 (-1.44)	-934.68 (-1.44)	-886.7 (-1.37)	-890.9 (-1.34)	44.70 (3.77)
Secondary School Education Enrolment (%) (1996-2012) Average				42.24 (1.50)	44.64 (1.58)	45.63 (1.62)	45.68 (-1.34)	-2.084 (-0.304)
Government Expenditure to GDP Ratio (%) (1996-2012) Average					-140.64 (-0.972)	-179.7 (-1.23)	-179.8 (-1.22)	3.518 (0.100)
Total Investment to GDP Ratio (%) (1996-2012) Average							-2.25 (-0.02)	84.82 (4.53)
GDP Per Capita 1996 at Constant 2005 USD in '000								1.104 (48.37)
Number of Observations	147	147	147	147	147	147	147	147
R^2	0.69	0.70	0.72	0.724	0.73	0.74	0.75	0.983

Note: Secondary Education Enrolment (%) represents the number of students enrolled in secondary education in percentage to the number of students in that official age group. For some of countries, this value is higher than 100 per cent, which means that some of the students enrolled in the secondary education are from outside the officially accepted age group.

Regression Table A-2.4 has no column heads as it is a waterfall representation with each successive column indicating results of regression analysis after an additional independent variable mentioned in the corresponding row is considered.

Source: Same as Annexure Table A-2.3.

Annexure Table A-2.5

GDP Per Capita Average (1996-2012) Regression of Various Groups of Economies

	Dependent Variable GDP Per Capita Average (1996-2012)				
	Low Income	*Lower Middle Income*	*Upper Middle Income*	*High Income*	*All Economies*
Constant	-47.496 (-0.521)	-450.38 (-2.09)	-1658.1 (-2.17)	-13333 (-2.34)	-3775.4 (-4.73)
Corruption Index (1996-2012) Average 0-10 Scale	281.22 (1.82)	329.04 (0.617)	287.30 (0.306)	65.18 (0.024)	304.7 (0.247)
Political Stability Index (1996-2012) Average 0-10 Scale	216.67 (1.47)	122.82 (0.67)	79.67 (0.881)	19.35 (0.15)	153.19 (1.013)
Voice and Accountability Index (1996-2012) Average 0-10 Scale	9.66 (0.529)	103.94 (0.105)	87.56 (1.47)	11.09 (2.30)	44.70 (3.77)
Secondary School Education Enrolment (%)(1996-2012) Average	0.739 (1.13)	4.862 (2.98)	5.07 (1.07)	-0.949 (2.30)	-2.084 (-0.304)
Government Expenditure to GDP Ratio (%) (1996-2012) Average	-3.04 (-1.809)	-9.08 (-1.31)	13.11 (0.46)	128.85 (0.901)	3.518 (0.100)
Total Investment to GDP ratio (%) (1996-2012) Average	5.44 (2.14)	12.89 (1.94)	42.20 (1.93)	170.32 (3.33)	84.82 (4.53)
GDP Per Capita 1996 at Constant 2005 $	0.811 (9.91)	1.12 (13.16)	0.845 (18.35)	1.11 (22.76)	1.104 (48.37)
Number of Observations	37	32	33	45	147
R^2	0.876	0.918	0.958	0.971	0.983

Note: Control of Corruption Index, Political Instability Index, and Voice and Accountability Index have been reported by the World Bank on a scale of -2.5 to +2.5. These indices have been converted to a scale to 0-10 with '0' representing the lower bound and '10' representing the upper bound. The formula used for scaling is the following:

Corruption/Political Instability/Voice and Accountability Index (0-10) Scale= [Corruption/Political Instability/Voice and Accountability Index (-2.5 to +2.5) Scale] *2.0 +5.0.

In all the three indices, '0' represents absolute corruption, absolute political instability and absolutely no freedom of expression while '10' represents no corruption, no political instability, and complete freedom of expression, respectively. These indices have been taken as arithmetic average during 1996-2012 period to wrinkle out yearly jumps/falls, if any. Data for these indices is from *World Bank Governance Indicators, 2012.*

Secondary Education Enrolment (%) represents the number of students enrolled in secondary education in percentage to the number of students in that official age group. For some of countries, this value is higher than 100 per cent, which means that some of the students enrolled in the secondary education are from outside the official age group. Data used in the analysis is arithmetic average of enrolment (%) during 1996-2012 period to wrinkle out yearly jumps/fall, if any. Data for this has been taken from the *World Bank Development Indicators, 2012*

Government Expenditure has been taken as percentage of GDP from the World Bank Development Indicators, 2012. It's used as arithmetic average during 1996-2012 period in the analysis to wrinkle out yearly jumps/falls, if any.

Investment has been taken as percentage of GDP from the IMF *World Economic Outlook, 2014*. It includes both public and private investment. It's used as arithmetic average during 1996-2012 period in the analysis to wrinkle out yearly jumps/falls, if any.

GDP, PPP (Purchasing power parity) Per Capita has been taken at constant 2005 $ from the *World Bank Development Indicator, 2012*. It's used as arithmetic average during 1996-2012 period in the analysis to wrinkle out yearly jumps/falls, if any.

Source: GDP Growth (%) from the World Bank; Investment/GDP ratio (%) involves both public and private investments; it is from IMF. Government Expenditure/GDP ratio (%) is from World Bank; Political Instability Index is from World Bank, and is on a scale of 0-10 (higher the index, lower the political instability). Corruption Index is from World Bank, and is on a scale of 0-10 (higher the index, lower the corruption). Voice and Accountability Index is from World Bank, and is on a scale of 0-10 (higher the index, higher the freedom of expression). GDP per capita is at constant 2005 $ and has been taken from the *World Bank Development Indicators, 2012*.

Annexure A-2.6

Expected GDP Per Capita during 1996-2012 when Countries Achieve Corruption Parity with Global Average and Scandinavian Countries

Country	*GDP Per Capita 1996-2012 Average at Constant 2005 USD*	*Expected GDP Per Capita Average 1996-2012 (Had the Corruption Index CPI been Equal to World Average, i.e., CPI=5.0)*	*Expected GDP Per Capita Average 1996-2012 (Had the Corruption Index CPI been Equal to that of Scandinavian Countries (9.0)*
India	746	1132	2928
China	1803	2212	4039
Bangladesh	423	1384	3179
Indonesia	1346	2065	3860
Pakistan	667	1516	3316
Brazil	4831	4853	6649

Note: Expected 1996-2012 numbers have been estimated using extrapolation when economies equal corruption index of world average and when economies achieve corruption levels of Scandinavian countries and continue to sustain those corruption levels for a period of 17 years as the regression analysis is done based on the average indices over a period of 17 years, i.e., 1996-2012.

Annexure A-2.7

Expected GDP Growth (%) during 1996-2012 when Countries Achieve Corruption Parity with Global Average and Scandinavian Countries

Country	*GDP Growth 1996-2012 Average*	*Expected GDP growth 1996-2012 (Had the Corruption Index CPI been Equal to World Average, i.e., CPI=5.0)*	*Expected GDP Growth 1996-2012 (Had the Corruption Index CPI been Equal to that of Scandinavian Countries (9.0)*
India	6.90%	7.06%	8.78%
China	9.71%	10.07%	11.51%
Bangladesh	5.72%	6.28%	7.88%
Indonesia	4.12%	4.47%	6.39%
Pakistan	3.85%	4.60%	6.20%
Brazil	2.95%	2.96%	2.96%

Note: Expected 1996-2012 numbers have been estimated using extrapolation when economies equal corruption index of world average and when economies achieve corruption levels of Scandinavian countries and continue to sustain those corruption levels for a period of 17 years as the regression analysis is done based on the average indices over a period of 17 years, i.e. 1996-2012.

3

Factors Impacting Corruption

The reasons of corruption in all global economies are fairly widespread and encompass both economic and social factors. In order to study these, it is essential that we try to see the influence of each one of these factors on degree of corruption. Many of these are also strongly related with each other. This causes problems in identifying the impact of each one of them separately. For example, as income rises, education levels also may go up. One of the major reasons of increase in per capita incomes is development of good institutions. The regulatory framework, therefore, also gets related to the incomes. There are number of other variables, which can thus be identified. Many of these improve as incomes rise. Partly, this growth in income is due to improvement in these factors themselves. This inter-relation in different parameters makes impact evaluation of each one of these individually on corruption a difficult task. We assess in this chapter impact of some key variables on corruption. We choose four categories of variables: income, poverty and income inequality; primary and secondary education; investment and government expenditure; and governance, including political stability and voice and accountability. We also look at fractionalisation of society and its impact on corruption. All these are treated as independent variables with an impact on corruption. We first take up how increase in income impacts corruption levels across the countries.

Income, Poverty and Income Inequality

It is generally accepted that as incomes rise, corruption levels go down. The increase in per capita income leads to less incentive for cutting corners or undertaking petty corruption activities to meet the basic requirements of life. It may not be so at all income levels. Using regression analysis, we study relation between per capita incomes and corruption in 161 countries for the period 1996-2012. For this we have used World Bank criterion of segregating world economies into four major income groups based on GNI (gross national income) per capita: low income, lower middle income, upper middle income and high income, similar to the classification used by us earlier and in later chapters.[1] The analysis indicates several features.

First, the relationship is quite significant when all the economies are considered together as manifested in strong R^2 and increasing values of corruption index with increase in income. Higher corruption index means lower corruption. It further establishes that with increase in incomes corruption goes down.

Second, for low income and lower middle income countries (GNI per capita less than or equal to $4,085), there is very little impact of income levels on corruption. These income levels act as a threshold below which incomes do not seem to impact corruption. At low income levels, aspirations of the people for development are not fully met. Irrespective of the society, therefore, in most of the countries, officials are prone to corrupt practices. When the per capita incomes are low, salary of a civil servant is also meagre. There may be unmet financial needs of individuals. Many of them resort to bribes through friends or agents, if they are able to manage this without great risk to themselves. Some others are willing to take risk and ask for bribes themselves. The low per capita incomes are not adequate for people who want to undertake political activity. Many of them, therefore, ask for political donations and are willing to trade their influence in policy making or in getting things done for people who are in a position to give them money. Political corruption, thus, thrives. The low incomes are generally associated with poor development of governance institutions. This gives an opportunity for government officials and politicians to make money, either in collusion or individually. In this age of globalisation and consumerism where the basic needs have been redefined, the citizen's aspirations are huge and low income levels are unable to meet them fully. Every opportunity is, therefore, seized by officials to meet these needs. There is no interest in simplifying procedure in civil service. In fact, rules are made more complicated so that transaction cost or bribery can be demanded. Corruption prevention and reduction in these economies are governed by factors other than per capita income: this may be political movement, civil society or good administration.

Third, impact of per capita income at upper middle income levels on corruption is more significant. At these income levels, with increase in income corruption tends to go down.

While the corruption is related to per capita income with lower corruption at high levels of per capita incomes, and vice-versa, there is also a strong impact of distribution of incomes on corruption. Inequality in income distribution leads to larger incentive for corruption. This works in several ways. First, sharp inequality leads to development of two classes of persons within the same country. There are citizens in first category, who have large wealth but are small in number. Their incentive for corruption is driven by greed and desire to further expand their wealth. The second category is of those whose asset base is small. In their case, the driving force for undertaking corrupt acts is improving the quality of life. Within this second category, there may be a large number of persons who may be below poverty line. The number of people below poverty line could be as high as 70 per cent. A number of African economies have large population below poverty line. This includes Zimbabwe with 72 per cent, Zambia 60.5 per cent, Togo 58.7 per cent, Sierra Leone 52.5 per cent and Chad with 46.5 per cent. Even in Latin America and Asia, there are a very large number of people living below poverty line.[2]

It is quite clear that if in any country one-third to half of the population is below poverty line, that country is living in two different worlds: one world is of those who have the resources and wealth and the other of those who are looking for getting basic necessities. In such a large division of a society, it is quite inevitable that there will be tensions and large incentives for corruption for those who are not able to meet their needs in a legitimate manner.

We have examined the relationship between corruption and poverty ratios. Data on poverty ratios from the World Bank were available only for 43 countries using which we carried out the analysis. In spite of poor compatibility of data due to different norms adopted by countries, we did this to get indicative results. The analysis confirms the hypothesis mentioned above that corruption increases as poverty goes up. Poorer nations are likely to have greater corruption. Our analysis indicates that an increase of 5 per cent in poverty results in 0.1 index value increase in corruption (Annexure Table A-3.1). These numbers may be purely indicative but the direction is very clear. Increased poverty does lead to increased corruption.

Similar situation exists in countries where income inequality is high. The level of income inequality is measured by income Gini coefficient.[3] Countries with low levels of inequality like Finland, Sweden, France and Switzerland have the value of this index below 0.30. On the contrary, Brazil with 0.53, China 0.47, South Africa 0.64 and Indonesia with 0.41 have high degree of inequality. The increase in inequality is likely to lead to increase in corruption. Larger inequality would lead to social stress. Large economic division in society is an ideal fertile ground for corrupt practices. Civil servants in such societies may take bribes and resort to corrupt practices to meet their needs. Data on income Gini coefficient from the World Bank is available only for 69 countries for various years using which we did the analysis to understand relationship between income inequality and corruption. We use the results more as an indicative measure of impact of inequality on corruption. We find a significant relationship between income inequality and corruption and estimate that an increase in inequality by 0.1 index value results into an increase in corruption index (0-10 scale) by 0.2. The results confirm our broad analysis that increasing inequality in society leads to higher corruption. Clearly, both poverty and inequality impact corruption.

Investment and Government Expenditure

While per capita income is an important characteristic on which corruption depends, the growth in income itself is highly dependent on investment in the economy as a share of GDP (gross domestic product). The income growth is also dependent on infrastructure development in that country. Such infrastructure in turn requires well-focused investment. It is, therefore, important that investments as a share of GDP are also considered as one of the factors which will have impact on corruption. This happens in several ways. First, political corruption may increase when such investments are sought to be made. In many countries, investments in the oil exploration blocks are under control of the government. It often results in bribes being demanded by officials who may be supported by the political bosses for whom it is primarily meant. Second, investments may be attractive for many investors as a business proposition. However, during the process of bid evaluation of the project, the civil servants in connivance with politicians may demand bribes for awarding contracts or not delaying papers for approval of proposal or speeding up decisions. Third, investments may require clearances which may be available subject to payment of bribe. These could relate to environment, land acquisition or other urban regulatory measures. In such cases, corruption results from giving of illegal benefits for getting a favourable decision or even a decision at all. There may be other instances also which all relate to investments in the economy. Larger the size of investment and poorer the climate for governance, higher is the bribe.

The regression analysis done by us, however, does not indicate any correlation between corruption and investment/GDP. It shows a very insignificant relation in different income groups in these two variables. With large increase in investments in the last 15 years, it seems difficult to accept a view that it makes no impact on corruption. It seems that data on political corruption does not get fully captured in current methods of developing corruption indices for countries.

Government expenditure in different countries has been expanding in the last few decades. As incomes rise, there is a demand for roads, hospitals, schools, irrigation dams, rural development projects and large purchases to meet the development needs. Large subsidies are given to identified groups to enable them to meet their basic needs and come up to the level of other social groups. This provides an opportunity for both politicians and civil servants to take bribes or siphon off money meant for poorer sections. At one point in time, exasperated with leakages in government expenditure, former Prime Minister of India, Rajeev Gandhi, had commented on leakages resulting in 85 per cent of the money being siphoned off by government officials and politicians.[4] Increasing government expenditure provides an opportunity for corruption. However, an analysis of the relationship between corruption and government expenditure does not support the thesis that larger expenditure leads to higher corruption. The analysis indicates that increase in government expenditure lowers corruption, albeit very marginally, possibly due to improvement in levels of education, health and infrastructure due to higher government expenditure. Corruption and government expenditure relationship is significant in all income groups except in the high income group. Here, too, it appears that a lot of corruption involved is not getting captured by corruption measuring agencies. This gap seems especially large in low income groups.

Political Stability and Voice and Accountability

Political stability is an important factor which impacts corruption. In several countries, regimes change for a variety of factors at a fast pace. In many countries, such changes take place because the governance institutions function in such a way that government is in office for a small period. This happens in countries like Italy, France, Japan, Pakistan and some Latin American countries. In many of the countries in Africa, this change is due to condition of civil war or regimes which are removed by force. Recently, in the case of Arab Spring, a number of countries had changes of regime due to people's movement.[5] This happened in the Middle East in Egypt, Iraq, Libya and Sudan. Recently, conditions in Ukraine are also such that the stability of the regime has come into question. Autocratic governments plagued by internal dissensions often get unstable. Recently, Thailand had one such situation.[6] Political instability leads to corruption. First, the control over the bureaucracy gets weakened and they start charging bribes. Second, the power equation in the countries is not very clear. Officials, therefore, start demanding bribes as it is not clear who is actually in charge for running the administration. Various groups take advantage of this situation. Third, different political groups who want to win in this inter-group rivalry start collecting money so that they are able to use it for winning the war against their rivals. In all such situations, the common man suffers. However, when the political stability is there, there is no guarantee that it will lead to low level of corruption. One of the classic examples is Russia, where the Mafia is strong. President Putin has been in power in varying capacities in Russia for a long time with a stable government. Corruption levels are still high.

Voice and accountability reflects people's control and say over the government's functioning. In democracies which are well-functioning and in countries of smaller population, like Switzerland, people have a say at local levels in governance matters. There is now a growing civil society which keeps a watch over many activities. However in larger size countries or where political institutions are not strong, this supervisory role of the people become weak. This institution level strength gives people a mechanism to keep a watch over corrupt politicians. The press joins in this in exposing the misdeeds. Nixon's act of misdemeanour was reported by *Washington Post* of the US. The corruption in Bofors case was highlighted by *The Hindu* newspaper of India.

We found in regression analysis a very strong correlation between corruption and the two independent variables: political stability, and voice and accountability. In all income groups, this relationship is strong and significant. Voice and accountability, however, has comparatively weaker relation in low and lower middle income groups. This reflects lack of effectiveness of these institutions in these economies. Political institution building and a strong press oversight is a must for controlling corruption. This will need to be built up in all countries.

Primary and Secondary Education

Education develops human values and is a powerful influence on it. In countries which have low incomes, it generally takes time to have good standards and universality. They have poor resources and are unable to invest adequately in social sectors. We consider the impact of education on corruption in two ways. First, we consider the impact of education in different income groups, e.g., low income, lower middle income, upper middle income and high income. We find that corruption is very poorly related with secondary education in low, lower middle and upper middle income groups. The average enrolment in these groups is 32.14 per cent, 62.04 per cent and 80.73 per cent respectively. With these levels of secondary enrolment, corruption is not dependent on levels of secondary school enrolment. In the high income group, where average of secondary school enrolment is 99 per cent, corruption shows a significant relationship with levels of secondary school enrolment.

We also take an alternative approach to consider this relationship. Based on secondary school enrolment levels, the entire universe of countries is divided in four quartiles: bottom 25 per cent, middle 25 per cent, upper middle 25 per cent and top 25 per cent. Thus, the first quartile contains countries with lowest level of secondary school enrolment. The highest quartile contains those countries which have the highest level of secondary school enrolment. For countries with lowest level of educational progress (the first quartile), the secondary school enrolment is 9.7-47.38 per cent. One would expect that with increase in share of these students, the levels of increased skills available after the secondary education would lead to higher growth and indirectly, therefore, also lower corruption. It is also likely that such increased education leads to more enlightened citizens who would be willing to discuss various issues and improve the level of institutional reforms. There is, however, practically no relationship between the secondary school enrolment and corruption for this quartile. Similar results are found for countries with increased levels of enrolment in the second quartile. While the bottom most 25 per cent of the countries in respect of secondary school enrolment show no relationship with corruption as mentioned above, the next quartile which has the average secondary school enrolment between 67.00 and 88.85 per cent also shows almost insignificant relationship with corruption. The next two quartiles of upper middle 25 per cent and top 25 per cent have secondary school enrolment of 89.05-97.94 per cent and 97.96-119.79 per cent respectively. In the highest quartile, enrolment is more than the universe of boys and girls of the age group. This indicates that the number of students who have crossed the concerned age group enrol themselves in the secondary school education due to their slow progress or their not being able to pass out in the age group (Annexure Table A-3.2).

As education levels start covering 90 per cent or more of students, which happens in top two quartiles, the influence of secondary education on corruption becomes manifest. In countries with enrolments lower than 90 per cent, there is insignificant relationship between corruption and levels of secondary school enrolment. We estimate that in countries which show secondary school enrolment beyond 90 per cent, 1 per cent increase in secondary school enrolment leads to 0.14 increase in corruption index (0-10 scale).

A feature of this relationship has wider implications. In countries of the first two quartiles (bottom 25% and middle 25%), income levels vary widely. There are countries in these groups which have income levels of $10,000 and above per annum. It is surprising that many of these countries with such high level of incomes have not paid attention to the universalisation of secondary education. Financial resource is clearly not the limiting factor. Policies need to be modified and focus of government expenditure changed to ensure universalisation of education at secondary school level.

The poor relation between corruption and secondary school education of countries where level of education is less than 80 per cent is possibly due to societal factors. When enrolment is low, the focus is on education *per se*. Parents would like their children to go to schools and study rather than pursue any other activity. Corruption is far from the minds of both students and parents. When sufficient numbers of students are going to secondary school, the focus may expand to other social problems. Since most of the students would be in secondary school, they may interact and discuss their future. If there is corruption in society, they may speak against it as it would hurt their careers. When the mass of such students is not large enough, the impact on corruption reduction may not be significant. It appears that 80 per cent of the student population is the critical mass required to address these issues.

We have also considered the relationship of corruption with primary education. We have studied enrolment levels in different group of economies, including OECD, African and Asian economies (Table 3.1).

Table 3.1

Primary Education Enrolment (%)

Group of Economies	*Average Enrolment in Primary School (%)*
All economies together	101.2
OECD economies	102.0
African economies	97.5
Asian Economies	102.8

Source: World Bank.

The level of primary school enrolment is fairly universal across all economies. In fact, there are many students who are not part of the age group and yet enrol themselves so as to complete primary education. Many students start their education late and get themselves enrolled as primary school education students. This is the basic level of education. It helps build a society which is making its citizens aware of their future needs and preparing them for economic growth and a better quality of life. It, however, does not lead to any worthwhile relationship with corruption. There is no impact on corruption in all categories of students in all economies. This is understandable. These children are in the age group 6-14 years and many of them are engaged only in the studies. To expect that they would be able to make impact on corruption, which requires institutional changes and reforms, is not reasonable. We feel that the thesis that primary education has an impact on corruption has, therefore, no basis.

Nature of Societies

The nature and composition of societies is part of the structure of a nation. Often countries have certain traditions. A large population may be influenced by their religious beliefs. There are discussions amongst families and in public debates on morality and the concept of Dharma. All these influence the extent of prevalent corruption. An important factor leading to higher level of corruption is the fractionalisation of societies. Globally many economies are ridden with factions, which are in themselves cohesive but work at cross-purposes with other groups in the society. In India, two levels of division are well accepted. First, one can consider the religion: Hindus, Muslims, Sikhs, Jains and Christians. Second, one can consider the caste. The

Mandal Commission has given a list of very large number of castes in India. The Backward Caste Commission Reports have identified more castes.[7] Each one of them tends to form a group. Each of these groups may tend to favour its cohort. If there are any allegations of corruption or wrong doing, the general tendency for such persons accused of these wrong doings is to try to get this settled politically through their kith and kin belonging to same caste or religion. This tendency is prevalent not only in India but is a global phenomenon.

In the US, there are a large number of groups which stick to each other and support one another. These include persons of Chinese origin, Italians, Indians, Mexicans, Russians, Polish and other such communities. Each one of these community tries to support each other. Similar situation exists in Russia, China, the UK and other countries. The ethno linguistic fractionalisation is measured by Mauro as follows:

$$\text{ELF} = 1 - \sum_{i=1}^{i} \left(\frac{n_i}{N}\right)^2, \qquad i = 1, \ldots, I,$$

where 'ELF' is Ethno Linguistic Fractionalisation (ELF) Index, 'N' is the population of ethnic or other groups and 'n_i' is the population of the ith group.[8]

This indicates that wherever there is only one community, n_i, which measures the fractions of community 'i' as against the total population, fractionalisation will be zero. As the fractionalisation increases and more and more communities are taken, the fractionalisation factor is positive but less than one. This is a very significant factor with impact on corruption in societies which have large populations from across the globe. We need to consider this.

Various studies have shown that women and older population have lesser patience with corrupt acts than others. Possibly, it may be the influence of religion in their lives, though there is no evidence to suggest this thesis.[9]

Governance

The social and economic conditions of the people, nature of society and education provide an ecosystem in which the institutions of governance function. The ecosystem may have citizens who are strongly opposed to corrupt behaviour. Larger their number, easier it is for the efficient functioning of governance system. Smaller proportion of such people in a society means need for very strong institutions of governance. These institutions have a key role in punishing the corrupt and preventing opportunities for corruption through systemic reforms. Some of the areas which need a closer look include anti-corruption laws and institutions for implementing them, political and economic institutions, judiciary, the media and the executive authority of the state and the way it is exercised. All these influence corruption levels very significantly.

Anti-corruption laws are framed by most economies. We have, however, no data for all global economies on nature of the laws, organisation responsible for administering it and efficacy of the process. Many countries have aligned their legislations to OECD Convention.[10] Several others have made very tough laws to promote investments in their economies. Some indications of the fact that countries have or are developing these organisations are available from the fact that UN Convention against Corruption (UNCAC) has been signed by 140 countries by May 2014. Since the Convention places a lot of obligations on the member states on anti-corruption measures and transparency, clearly there is a widespread movement to set up anti-corruption institution.[11] It is, however, not possible to assess the efficacy of anti-corruption organisations. An indication of this is available from the fact that corruption in most of the countries has reduced very marginally over the last 15 years.

Strong political institutions including the parliament and state legislature, holding of regular elections, strong local bodies and effective participation of different sections of society in political process are essential for lowering corruption. The nature of political leaders who have the power to take decisions is a very critical factor.[12] The ecosystem and people's movement against corrupt behaviour greatly influence this. Both political stability and voice and accountability, to which we referred earlier, are manifestation of strength of political institutions. If governments are not stable, the politicians may offer bribes to parliamentarians to save their governments and continue to enjoy political power. These instances were reported in 1990s in India and in Italy. The quality of local administration and decentralisation of administrative and financial powers play an important part in determining corruption levels. In India, for example, there is a large degree of transfer of resources at local levels to village *panchayats*, district *panchayats* and block development committees. It has given rise to enormous corruption as these institutions are not governing themselves well and the quality of these is generally not good. These reforms have to be addressed to have lower corruption.

A number of other institutions also have large impact on corruption. These relate to administrative procedures, economic policies, judiciary, police and the media. Most of them need major reforms. In 2005, lower judiciary and police in India was assessed by Transparency International (TI) as very corrupt. In many countries, the police have very high level of corruption. Judicial courts have large pendency. In India, it is estimated that nearly 30 million cases are pending in the courts. So while the system of administering justice is excellent with Supreme Court at the apex level, one is not sure of getting decisions on property and economic matters expeditiously. This is the breeding ground of corruption as alternative avenues are explored when laws in the normal course do not provide expeditious justice.

Government procedures for availing public services are often very cumbersome. This provides opportunity for corruption to government officials. It is useful to look at an example to have a fuller appreciation of the problem. The World Bank has prepared an index on ease of doing business. This is measured by a whole range of parameters by the World Bank. In their report for the year 2014, they have made a study of 189 countries, and studied ease of doing business. The report has undertaken study of following issues: starting a business, dealing with construction permits, getting electricity, registering property, getting credit, protecting investors, paying taxes, trading across borders, enforcing contracts and resolving insolvency. The assessment made by the World Bank in the above areas thus indicates the difficulty in doing business. For measuring these, they undertake four components for starting the business: number of procedures involved, number of days per procedure, annual income per capita and minimum capital requirement for opening the business. The average is then taken of the percentile in which the country is in these four areas. Similar average is done for other business areas like dealing with construction permits and so on. Based on the above, they have constructed an index which is indicative of difficulty of doing business. In case there are difficulties in transacting business, the business investor invariably may resort to offering bribes. The ease of doing business index is, therefore, a good surrogate for petty corruption. This involves generally all business dealings where new businesses may offer bribes to government officials and politicians. If the systems are such that the procedures are simple and not time consuming, the incentive for offering bribes does not exist. In such cases, therefore, both the civil servant and the politician cannot hope to get bribes. However if the procedure is complex, as indicated by a very high index value and correspondingly higher rank in the inter-country ranking, the incentive is very much in existence both for the government official and the politician.[13]

The ease of doing business, however, does not cover petty corruption in other regulatory dealings of the government: police, judiciary, municipal services, certificates required from the government, public distribution system (PDS), giving financial assistance to individuals, electric connections, passports and similar other facilities. But the index gives a good assessment of the degree of administrative inefficiency or problems which in turn are reasons for corruption. It can be used as a surrogate measure for the above deficiencies as well. Generally, inefficiencies in the large area of doing business should move in tandem with inefficiencies in other areas of government inefficiencies.

Press acts as a watchdog on corruption. If it gets bought over by business interests as is happening in the Indian media, the oversight may become weak. Independent press is an institution which is a major bulwark against corruption.[14]

It is difficult to find a measure for index of governance. The World Bank has prepared an index which includes corruption itself as one component. It includes political stability and voice and accountability as part of the strength of political institutions. It uses, in addition, regulatory quality, government effectiveness and rule of law. We consider corruption and political institutions independently and take the average of the other three. This we treat as Modified Governance Index. It reflects the nature and quality of the institutions of governance. This is used by us to consider impact on corruption in our regression analysis. We find a very strong correlation between the two. Of all the variables considered so far, its impact on corruption is highest. In different income groups, it shows varying degree of correlation. While in high and upper middle income countries it exhibits a strong impact, in low and lower middle income countries, its impact is comparatively weak. Political stability has a comparable impact in these countries. All these indices impact corruption levels very strongly in global economies. (Annexure Table A-3.3)

Notes and References

1. Each year on 1 July, The World Bank revises the classification of the world's economies based on estimates of GNI per capita for the previous year. The updated GNI per capita estimates are also used as input to the Bank's operational classification of economies, which determine their lending eligibility. As of 1 July 2013, the World Bank income classifications by GNI per capita are as follows: Low income: $1,035 or less; Lower middle income: $1,036 to $4,085; Upper middle income: $4,086 to $12,615; and High income: $12,616 or more.
2. *World Bank Development Indicators, 2012.*
3. Gini index measures the extent to which the distribution of income or consumption expenditure among individuals or households within an economy deviates from a perfectly equal distribution. A Lorenz curve plots the cumulative percentages of total income received against the cumulative number of recipients, starting with the poorest individual or household. The Gini index measures the area between the Lorenz curve and a hypothetical line of absolute equality, expressed as a percentage of the maximum area under the line. Thus a Gini index of 0 represents perfect equality, while an index of 1.0 implies perfect inequality.
4. Rajiv Gandhi, the sixth Prime Minister of India, once mentioned in the mid-1980s that "out of every rupee spent by the government only 15 paise (100 paisa = 1 rupee) reaches the poor."
5. The Arab Spring is a revolutionary wave of demonstrations and protests (both non-violent and violent), riots and civil wars in the Arab world that began on 18 December 2010 and spread throughout countries of the Arab League and surroundings. While the wave of initial revolutions and protests had expired by mid-2012, some refer to the ongoing large-scale conflicts in Middle East and North Africa as a continuation of the Arab Spring, while others refer to the second wave of revolutions and civil wars post 2012 as the Arab Winter.
6. On 22 May 2014, the Royal Thai Armed Forces led by General Prayuth Chanocha, Commander of the Royal Thai Army (RTA), launched a coup against the caretaker government of Thailand, following six months of political crisis. The military established a *junta* called National Council for Peace and Order (NCPO) to govern the nation.
7. National Commission for Backward Classes is an Indian Statutory Body established on 14 August 1993, under the provisions of National Commission for Backward Classes Act,

1993 (Act No. 27 of 1993). The commission considers inclusions in and exclusions from the lists of communities notified as backward for the purpose of job reservations and tenders the needful advice to the Central Government as per Section 9(1) of the NCBC Act, 1993. Similarly, the states have also constituted commissions for BCs. As of 24 July 2014, over 2,000 groups have been listed as OBCs. Both the National Commission for Backward Classes and National Commission for Scheduled Castes have the same powers as a Civil Court.

8. Mauro, P. (1995). "Corruption and Growth", *The Quarterly Journal of Economics* 110(3): 681–712. MIT Press.
9. Strate, J.M., C.J. Parrish, C.D. Elder and C. Ford III (1989). "Life Span Civic Development and Voting Participation", *American Political Science Review* 83(2): 443-64; See also: Swamy, A., Stephen Knack, Y. Lee, Omar Azfar (2000). "Gender and Corruption", *CDE Working Paper Series*. MA, USA: Williams College, Centre for Development Economics.
10. The OECD Anti-Bribery Convention (officially Convention on Combating Bribery of Foreign Public Officials in International Business Transactions) is a convention of the OECD aimed at reducing corruption in developing countries by encouraging sanctions against bribery in international business transactions carried out by companies based in the Convention member countries. Its goal is to create a truly level playing field in today's international business environment.
11. The UNCAC is a multilateral convention negotiated by members of the United Nations (UN). It is the first global legally binding international anti-corruption instrument. In its 71 articles divided into 8 chapters, UNCAC requires that State Parties implement several anti-corruption measures which may affect their laws, institutions and practices. These measures aim at preventing corruption, criminalising certain conducts, strengthening international law enforcement and judicial cooperation, providing effective legal mechanisms for asset recovery, technical assistance and information exchange, and mechanisms for implementation of the Convention, including the Conference of the State Parties (CoSP) to the UNCAC.The UN Office on Drugs and Crime (UNODC) promotes the convention and its implementation. UNCAC was adopted by the UN General Assembly on 31 October 2003 by Resolution 58/4. It was opened for signature in Merida, Yucatan, Mexico, from 9–11 December 2003 and thereafter at UN headquarters in New York City. It was signed by 140 countries. As of April 2014, there are 171 parties, including the European Union (EU).
12. Chowdhury, S.K. (2004). "The Effect of Democracy and Press Freedom on Corruption: An Empirical Test", *Economics Letters* 85: 93-101; See also: Treisman, D. (2000). "The Causes of Corruption: A Cross-national Study", *Journal of Public Economics* 76: 399-457.
13. Ease of doing business ranks economies from 1 to 189, with first place being the best. A high ranking (a low numerical rank) means that the regulatory environment is conducive to business operation. The index averages the country's percentile rankings on 10 topics covered in the World Bank's Doing Business. The ranking on each topic is the simple average of the percentile rankings on its component indicators.
14. Brunetti, A. and B. Weder (2003). "A Free Press is Bad News for Corruption", *Journal of Public Economics* 87: 1801-24. See also: Vogl, F. (1999). "Curbing Corruption: The Media's Work—Recommendations for Action", *Transparency International Working Paper.* Presented at the 9th IACC; Suphachalasai, S. (2005). "Bureaucratic Corruption and Mass Media", *Environmental Economy and Policy Research, Discussion Paper Series Number* 05.2005. University of Cambridge.

Annexure Table A-3.1

Average (1996-2012) Corruption versus Average (1996-2012) Secondary Education Regression at Different Levels of Income (Corruption is a dependent variable and Secondary Education is an independent variable)

Countries	*Income Level*	*Constant*	*Secondary Education Enrolment (%)*	*Total Number of Observations*	R^2
Low income countries	Income level than $1,035	3.83076 (9.206)	-0.0093 (9.206)	28	0.044
Lower middle income countries	Income level per capita, $1,036-$ 4,085	3.4516 (4.156)	0.00649 (0.6502)	29	0.015
Upper middle income countries	Income level per capita, $4,086-$12,615	0.93202 (0.4341)	0.0440 (1.885)	25	0.133
High income countries	Income level per capita, $12,616 or more	4.40166 (1.983)	0.03031 (1.404)	33	0.59
All countries		1.5824 (3.232)	0.04325 (7.491)	115	0.33

Note: Figures in bracket indicate t values.

Annexure Table A-3.2

Average (1996-2012) Corruption versus Average (1996-2012) Secondary Education Regression at Different Levels of Secondary Enrolment (Corruption is a dependent variable and Secondary Education is an independent variable)

	Classification of Countries Based on Secondary School Enrolment			
	Bottom 25%	*Middle 25%*	*Upper Middle 25%*	*Top 25%*
Constant	3.1848 (5.697)	5.0465 (1.601)	-2.698 (-0.2177)	-8.2884 (-1.19)
Secondary Enrolment	0.00811 (0.6109)	-0.008586 (-0.271)	0.08823 (0.6743)	0.1412 (2.133)
R^2	0.014	0.081	0.17	0.34
Secondary Enrolment Range	14.7%-65.1%	67.00%-88.85%	89.05%-97.94%	97.96%-119.79%
Average GDP per capita	$791	$7,678	$14,962.4	$24,322.5
GDP per capita Range	$153.4-$2,685.8	$458.6-$70, 592.2	$1,629.6-$54,995.9	$845.8-$77,971.2

Note: t valuations are in bracket.

Annexure A-3.3

Corruption Regression of Various Income Groups

	Low Income Group	*Lower-middle Income Group*	*Upper-middle Income Group*	*High Income Group*	*All Income Groups*
Corruption *versus* Investment/GDP Ratio (%) 1996-2012 average					
Constant	2.7735 (5.426)	2.43227 (6.775)	3.882 (4.26)	8.888 (16.8)	5.09 (10.92)
Investment/GDP ratio (%) 1996-2012 average	0.0362 (1.37)	0.05847 (4.009)	0.0308 (0.8392)	-0.070 (-3.622)	-0.00412 (-0.2173)
R^2	0.0627	0.34	0.021	0.233	0.0003
Corruption *versus* Government Expenditure/GDP Ratio (%) 1996-2012 Average					
Constant	2.89 (10.19)	3.164 (9.434)	3.162 (4.60)	5.34 (4.972)	2.54 (5.649)
Government Expenditure/GDP ratio (%) 1996-2012 average	0.04349 (2.183)	0.0456 (2.058)	0.09387 (2.218)	0.1019 (1.771)	0.1586 (5.79)
R^2	0.15	0.12	0.13	0.067	0.19
Corruption *versus* Secondary Education (%) 1996-2012 Average					
Constant	3.81 (14.99)	4.005 (10.69)	3.5122 (5.346)	-0.1007 (-0.074)	2.112 (6.682)
Secondary School Enrolment (%) 1996-2012 average	-0.0112 (-1.612)	-0.00309 (-0.5629)	0.0149 (1.777)	0.0736 (5.423)	0.0407 (9.976)
R^2	0.084	0.01011	0.087	0.41	0.41
Corruption *versus* Per Capita GDP 1996-2012 Average					
Constant	3.51 (9.415)	3.694 (11.71)	3.335 (8.445)	5.091 (13.89)	3.883 (35.14)
Per Capita GDP average 1996-2012 at constant 2005 $ in '000	-0.1638 (-0.1761)	0.0907 (0.3932)	0.2869 (3.635)	0.0808 (6.71)	0.115 (18.09)
R^2	0.0011	0.0049	0.2859	0.511	0.698
Corruption *versus* Political Instability Index 1996-2012 Average 0-10 Scale					
Constant	2.42 (8.63)	2.65 (7.54)	2.059 (4.137)	0.7484 (0.6644)	0.7748 (2.624)
Political Instability Index 0-10	0.3039 (3.95)	0.2966 (3.433)	0.5496 (5.399)	1.0092 (5.811)	0.8877 (15.25)
R^2	0.36	0.28	0.47	0.44	0.62

contd...

...contd...

	Corruption *versus* Voice and Accountability Index 1996-2012 Average 0-10 Scale				
Constant	2.65 (6.12)	3.261 (6.622)	1.7805 (3.866)	1.35 (1.759)	0.6466 (2.472)
Voice and Accountability Index 0-10	0.2309 (1.922)	0.1356 (1.147)	0.5699 (6.643)	0.858 (7.769)	0.877 (17.69)
R^2	0.12	0.040	0.57	0.58	0.69
	Corruption *versus* Governance Index 1996-2012 Average 0-10 Scale				
Constant	1.614 (3.684)	0.3971 (0.7684)	0.1641 (0.4527)	-1.99 (-4.505)	-0.1338 (-0.9421)
Voice and Governance Index 0-10	0.5561 (4.307)	0.857 (6.654)	0.9301 (12.65)	1.2749 (21.1)	1.0158 (38.51)
R^2	0.40	0.59	0.83	0.91	0.913
Constant					50.8789 (17.08)
	Corruption Average (1996-2012) *versus* Gini Coefficient (2011) Regression				
Gini Coefficient					-2.0124 (-3.655)
Number of Observations					69
R^2					0.17
	Average (1996-2012) Corruption *versus* Poverty Ratio (%) (2011) at US$1.25/day at PPP Regression				
Constant					4.26005 (25.93)
Coefficient					-0.0231 (-2.618)
Number of Observations					43
R^2					0.143

Note: Higher the corruption index, lower the corruption. Higher the voice and accountability index, higher the freedom of expression. Higher the political instability index, lower the political instability. Governance index is the average of government effectiveness index, rule of law index and regulatory quality index. All governance indices are on a scale of 0-10, p values for all cases <0.05. Poverty headcount is in percentage measures, percentage of population earning less than $ 1.25/day at PPP. Gini coefficient is in percentage and represents inequality, i.e., '0' means no inequality and '1' means perfect inequality.

4

International Experience

All national economies are affected by corruption in some measure. They have, therefore, reformed their institutions and put up checks and balances in the governance system to reduce corruption and improve governance. Not all of them have set up anti-corruption agencies, as in Singapore and Hong Kong. But they have various institutions and laws to address the problem of corruption. At a global level, they have combined to evolve a common platform against corruption through the United Nations (UN) system. Most of them have laws defining bribery and set up machinery to punish those who violate these. The nature of anti-corruption agencies in different countries is different as some have single agency system like Singapore, Hong Kong, etc., while the likes of the US, India and Finland have multi-agency systems (Meagher, 2004)[1] (Annexure Tables A-4.1 and A-4.2). We, in this chapter, have analysed the nature and causes of political corruption amongst some major developed economies. We, however, start with the UN Convention against Corruption (UNCAC), a major UN initiative to address this issue.

The UNCAC was conceived in the backdrop of growing concerns in the international community on corruption and need for cooperation amongst global economies to control its expansion. After extensive debate, the UN recognised the need for a convention in December 2000. It, however, took several years before the member countries could agree to details of such a convention document. Finally, it was approved in October 2003 and put up for signatures and approvals or ratification. The documents require at least 40 countries to sign it before it could come into effect. Finally, when it came into effect in December 2005, 140 countries had signed and ratified the documents. India was among those which signed it in December 2005 itself. It, however, took some time for it to ratify the conventions which was finally done in May 2011. It is a failure of our policy making system that we took six years to ratify the Convention. While the official version indicated that a ministerial committee was looking into it, the fact remains that the ratifications was done immediately after the movement against corruption had gained strength in the country and Anna Hazare (India's anti-corruption crusader) had started his fast at Jantar Mantar in April 2011. The Convention was signed by April 2014, or ratified as required by each country's laws by 171 countries. The Convention includes model policies on prevention of corruption. These cover establishment of anti-corruption bodies, transparency in financing of election campaigns, and measures by countries to trace, seize and confiscate the proceeds of corruption. The convention requires countries to frame laws to make different types of corrupt acts a criminal offence. The extent of criminality attached to various acts of commission or omission is expected to cover a very wide set of such acts. The convention also expects countries to cooperate with each other in fighting against corruption, including prevention, investigations and prosecution of offenders. It requires member countries to render assistance to each other in gathering and transferring information for use in court. The convention provides for assistance in recovery of proceeds of corrupt acts which is stated as a basic policy. Recovery of money transferred by corrupt people in India and stashed abroad in Swiss banks or other banks or in other ways is covered in this manner. The convention is fairly wide in its scope and covers both public and private players. A lot of provisions are part of good governance practices and provide for setting up of anti-corruption institutions which have fully trained staff and financial support from the government to meet their requirements. The parties to the convention are obliged to facilitate merit in recruitment of public servants and prescribe the code of conduct for them while in service. Such a conduct includes disclosure of financial interest. It also provides for fighting corruption with the help of community support and focuses on transparent functioning of the government, with civil society acting as a watchdog. To further strengthen the mechanism, it was decided to set up a review mechanism. The convention has helped the creation of positive environment against corruption. It provides a forum for civil society to monitor the government and put debates on corruption in centre stage. While it is difficult to claim that corruption has gone down globally as a result of these efforts, this initiative by international community to clean the global system has encouraged countries to focus on governance and reduce corruption.

Finland

The country has been very successful in fighting corruption and has some unique features. It has a population of 5.5 million and been ranked third in the Corruption Perception Index (CPI) of 2013.[2] The country had a per capita income of $47,219 in 2013.[3] The high level of incomes and social security measures which envisage free education, pension from the state above the age of 65 years and free medical care have left very little incentive for people to indulge in corrupt acts. This was not always so. The country was relatively poor and vulnerable to shocks. The economy was predominantly agrarian and in 1950, half the population was dependent upon primary sector. Fast economic growth over the last five decades has led to increased incomes and high standards of living.[4]

Several factors have contributed to the low level of corruption. The Finnish society is very egalitarian. In 1906, it approved right to vote and stand for elections both for men and women. It was the first country in the world to do so. It has evolved good administrative institutions. During 1100-1809 AD, it was under Swedish rule and subsequently under Russia as a grand duchy. Over all, in these years, the law which evolved had its roots in the local customs which led to great respect for it. The society then was basically law-abiding. This was also reflected in its civil service. The service had people who had been educated in law in a university. This tradition of legal background continued. The administrators were always highly respected in the society and very well paid. The recruitment was based on merit. The civil servants were at the head of ministries till 2005. The service valued its respect. In the country with a small population, any corruption by a civil servant would be talked about. They did not want to sully their image. A clean civil service helped in lowering corruption. Several other features of Finnish society and its political structure are unique and have ensured a very low level of corruption. Considering the corruption involved in raising finances, Finland was one of the few countries to provide for state funding of political parties. An important and very distinguishing feature of the Finnish administrative system is the referendary system of governance prevalent in the country. This ensures clean decision-making. A referendary is a civil servant who prepares the basic note on any issue and makes his recommendations. Ministers have a right to disagree with him, but the responsibility of such decision is that of the minister. The civil servant has a right to disagree with him and can put this in his note which is rarely done. If the referendary does not agree with the decision, he can record it and in all such cases the responsibility for decision lies with the minister. This makes it difficult for the minister to indulge in corrupt practice. Some of the other unique features of the governance are: First, collective decision-making is preferred. It may be easy to approach one individual and offer him bribes. It becomes very difficult when a number of people are involved. To convince so many people is difficult and fraught with risk. There is a danger that one person may blow the whistle. In all such cases, principle of objectivity is kept in view by those taking part in decision-making. This requires that in any matter where there is conflict of interest due to his family or his own relationship, the official concerned does not participate or deal with a subject. Second, an oversight is kept by the chancellor of justice and parliamentary ombudsmen who are officers appointed by the president, These institutions are highly respected. They can investigate into any case of complaint received by them. They tour the areas and look at the performance of various institutions. They work independently. These institutions have helped develop a strong influence on the level of honesty and conduct of officials. Third, transparency and openness in decision taking is a key principle of governance. Decisions are made public and are open for scrutiny to the people at large. Open access to public records makes it possible for individuals and association to oversee the exercise of authority by government officials and to judge whether there was any mischief involved in the transaction.

The laws on bribery recognise active bribery and passive bribery. Such types of offences are prevalent in private business too. Certain offences committed by public officials are also part of the criminal law which includes provision on bribery. However, these acts are not considered to be corruption and are termed as misconduct. The corruption levels in Finland are low but two areas of corruption have been commented upon. First, the 'old boys' network based corruption has been noticed. In a small population with small size of cities, officials work for long years. They know the population. Many of the private contractors know the officials as they have been with them in the school or are members of some organisation. In such cases, when contract is awarded to them, even when on merit, it becomes difficult to decide about the fairness of such award. There is in such cases a suspicion lurking that the 'old boys' network is active and results in favours. Second, in international trade in a number of countries, bribe had to be paid. Finland has borders with Russia. A large number of their companies have trading relations across the borders. In such cases, instances of corruption have been noticed.[5]

The Finnish society has low level of corruption. The civil services, egalitarian nature of society, transparency, the system of parliamentary ombudsman and chancellor of justice have helped lower the level of corruption. However, very high levels of per capita incomes which are 30 times in nominal terms and 7 times in (PPP) purchase price parity terms of India have de-incentivised corruption. A small and intimate society with fear of public exposure has helped promotion of honest behaviour.

United States of America

Efforts made to control corruption in the US have significance for major global economies like India and China. These countries compare well in the size of economies in terms of PPP and complexity of governance. Experience of the US can be a major input in policy making for controlling corruption in these countries. The US has, however, a per capita income which is 10 times that of India in PPP terms and 30 times in nominal US$ terms. The higher per capita incomes have enabled it to provide a good standard of living to its citizens, excellent infrastructure, social benefits and health care facilities which India with its current income levels is not able to provide. These levels of income de-incentivise corruption in the US. However, the large income inequalities act as a negative factor. The Gini coefficient, a measure of inequality of incomes, is 0.47. This is considered fairly high amongst the major global economies.[6] This leads to a negative impact on standards of integrity in the country, especially at grass-roots levels. Petty corruption in the US is very minimal. An indication of this is the US rank in ease of doing business which was 4.0 in 2013 amongst more than 150 nations.[7] This indicates that procedures for setting up business, approvals required from government authorities and other related procedures do not take time. Most of these activities take place at a local level and reflect the overall efficiency of the system.

The US measures against corruption are primarily aimed at developing ethical norms for public servants, eliminating corrupt practices from international business and reducing high level corruption or political corruption or grand corruption. Corruption of federal employees is covered by a series of legislations, some of which were not originally intended for this purpose. Such acts include the Hobbs Act enacted in 1934, Mail and Wire Frauds Act enacted in 1872, Travel Act enacted in 1961, and Racketeer Influenced and Corrupt Organisation Act, 1970.[8] Through an interpretation of various provisions, courts have made them applicable to federal officials and corrupt politicians in certain situations. Recent legislations which directly address bribery include Federal Official Bribery and Gratuity statute 18 USC 201 and criminal conflict of interest statutes 18 USC 202-209 were enacted in 1962, the Foreign Corrupt Practices Act 1977, and Federal Programme Bribery Statute 18 USC 666 enacted in 1984. The nature of offence covered by 18 USC 201 includes both accepting and giving bribes. The definition of public official is very wide and includes congressmen. Later in 1984, it was expanded to persons including agents of organisations getting federal grant of more than $10,000.[9] The problem of raising funds for campaign financing and corruption involved in it remains unresolved. Recently, in a judgement of the US Supreme Court, it has been held that for financing political activities, no restrictions can be put on companies. They can finance any number of candidates or fund political parties.

After the Watergate scandal, two important legislations came into effect: the Foreigners Corrupt Practice Act (FCPA) 1977 and Ethics in Governance Act (1978).[10] The FCPA was a law to stop corruption and bribery in securing contracts and other business by the US firms in different countries. The Act prohibits the US companies and persons from making payments to foreign officials or politicians for obtaining or retaining a business. The provisions of the act were subsequently in 1998 made applicable to foreign firms and persons who do these prohibited activities while in the US. A very broad definition of foreign officials has been adopted to make the provisions stringent. The other part of the law amended the US Securities Exchange Act 1934 to make filling of reports mandatory for certain payments to foreign officials or other foreign firms and to maintain an account for this purpose. The act has thus put stringent restrictions on payment of bribes to foreign companies.

The other major initiative was in the wake of Watergate scandal with President Nixon firing Archibald Cox, the special counsel investigating the affair. The Ethics in Government Act was passed in 1978 with the approval of Jimmy Carter, the then US President. It has provisions for full financial disclosure by all federal officials and persons whose appointment is approved by the US senate. Filling of such financial disclosures is also necessary for the President and the Vice President apart from the US public official nominees to positions which require senate confirmation and judges. The Act also provided for setting up of an office of government ethics which was initially a part of the office of Personnel Management, but in 1989 was moved as an independent office with a Director of Ethics. The Director was appointed by the President of the US and had access to all the records. He advises on the implementation of provisions of financial transparency. The Act also gives right to any person to access such financial disclosure acts, except for prohibited usage. Such prohibited usage included use for commercial purposes, use for making credit ratings and similar other purposes. The record were available for inspection 15 days after the filling for which a fixed time limit was prescribed within which these were to be available. The Act also provides for limitation on income additional to employment. This prohibition has been widely resented by many. However, the US Supreme Court in the US *versus* National Treasury Employees Union has held that lower level officials can accept money for their non-political unofficial writings as honoraria. For senior officials, the court held that salary increases were quite enough to offset such honoraria.[11]

Several states have passed laws on disclosure by government officials, similar to Federal law. These include California and New York, which have strict laws but others like Florida, Pennsylvania and Alabama have also passed similar laws.

The Ethics in Government Act, 1978, also provided for a special prosecutor to be appointed for investigating cases of corruption. On receipt of complaints against President or Vice President or other specified category of officials, the Attorney General would look into it and send a report to the US Supreme Court who then consider it. The report had to be given on whether the charges were accepted or rejected. In case, the allegations were found to be true, the court appointed a special prosecutor and decided its limit of work. The prosecutor was appointed by a bench of three judges which were decided by the Supreme Court. The special prosecutor could not be removed by the Attorney General except on grounds of mental disability or such other situations. While the institution of a special counsel was in existence even earlier, with the passage of the 1978 Act, it got special legal sanction. The primary objective for providing this legal sanction appears to have been to avoid the conflict of interest as the Attorney General was himself an appointee of the government. The provisions of the special prosecutor had a sunset clause according to which after five years these provisions needed renewal. There were worries in the Executive that the special prosecutors were extremely powerful and could not be removed easily. This power had been taken over under the act by the Supreme Court. It seems that there were reservations in the congress on these issues. Finally, after several extensions of this provision, in 1999 it was decided not to grant any further extension. The decisions on prosecution are now being taken by the Department of Justice.

The Director of Government Ethics, though a small institution, is extremely powerful in its advice on various ethical standards and especially on financial disclosure statements. It undertakes education for the employees on ethical standards. It has further to ensure that conflict of interest is avoided in all transactions. In the event, if it comes across any instance where criminal investigation is required, it hands it over to the concerned agencies, as it does not have power to investigate cases itself. There are several other institutions who take action when in cases of corruption are referred. These include public corruption unit of Federal Bureau of Investigation (FBI), the Department of Justice, congressional committees and general accounting offices.

Singapore

A country with a colonial past, Singapore had huge corruption in the 1940s and 1950s.[12] In 1952, it set up the Corrupt Practices Investigation Bureau. It was initially put in Attorney General's chamber. In 1959, when Singapore gained independence, it was moved to Prime Minister's Office. It has remained there since then. Earlier, the task of prevention of corruption was assigned to a small anti-corruption unit in the police.[13] The Prevention of Corruption Act was amended in 1960s and subsequently several times.

The anti-corruption strategy of Singapore had two phases. In the first phase, emphasis was on reform of system and procedures and effective implementation of the provisions of the Prevention of Corruption Act 1960. The People's Action Party (PAP) was in power all along during this period and Prime Minister Lee Kuan Yew worked on this with a firm hand. It is interesting to note that though Singapore has a parliamentary form of government with separate legislature (unicameral), judiciary and the executive, the separation of powers is weak. The power of legislations is with both the executive and the legislature. The courts thus generally take a pro-government stand. In this environment, the first phase was implemented and helped reduction of corruption. After success in the first phase, the strategy in second phase was to increase the salaries of government servants and ministers to a very high level, so that they become immune to corruption and have no incentive to adopt corrupt practices. This strategy still continues. In 2007, Singapore announced hike in the salary of its Prime Minister to 3.1 million Singapore dollars as against $400,000 of the US President.[14] The increase in salaries acted as an icing on the cake. The graft had reduced substantially in the first phase itself. Measures in phase II further cemented the process.

The Director of the Corrupt Practices Investigation Bureau (CPIB) is appointed by the President but can be removed at will of the executive. He is in that respect not immune from executive pressure. The CPIB has the power to conduct investigations in all cases of graft and file charges in the court. It has police powers of search and seizure. Prosecution, however, is done by public prosecutors. During the course of investigation, the CPIB can look at bank accounts, search the books of banks and look into assets of the concerned official as well as members of his family. It is, however, a comparatively small unit. Officers for CPIB are not from the police and recruited from outside.

The definition of illegal gratification under Section 3 of the Prevention of Corruption Act is fairly wide. 'Gratification' includes:

(a) Money or any gift, loan, fee, reward, commission, valuable security or other property or interest in property of any description, whether movable or immovable.

(b) Any office, employment or contract.

(c) Any payment, release, discharge or liquidation of any loan, obligation or other liability whatsoever, whether in whole or in part.

(d) Any other service, favour or advantage of any description whatsoever, including protection from any penalty or disability incurred or apprehended or from any action or proceedings of a disciplinary or penal nature, whether or not already instituted, and including the exercise or forbearance from the exercise of any right or any official power or duty; and

(e) Any offer, undertaking or promise of any gratification within the meaning of paragraphs (a), (b), (c) and (d).

The Act provides for punishment up to seven years and fine.

An important part of CPIB functions is to look at corruption in private sector, and by members of parliament (MPs). The Act of 1960 (as amended) states that for corrupt acts, MPs are liable for punishment in the same way as others. Further, the presumption is against the offender, whether he was in a position to meet the commitment made by him under the promised corrupt act or not. Whether he was in a position or entitled to take that decision or not is not relevant if he has received gratification.

Hong Kong

Hong Kong, a British Colony till 1997, had a very high degree of corruption four decades back. Then there were public protests and that changed it all. The events leading to it were described by *South China Morning Post* of February, 2013:[15]

> In the summer of 1973 decorated Police Chief Superintendent Peter Fitzroy Godber could see the writing on the wall. The London native had spent more than two decades living in Hong Kong, a city where institutionalized corruption penetrated every strata of society. Bribes known as "tea money" were paid for basic services, from getting a home phone installed to making sure firefighters showed up when there was a blaze. Police officers of all ranks had accepted payoffs for decades. In 1971, an internal police unit discovered an unusual remittance from Hong Kong to Canada; C$12,000 had been transferred to a Canadian Bank account under the name "P.F. Godber". Police launched an internal investigation, code named "Havana". But with limited powers, the anti-corruption unit made little progress. Godber applied for early retirement, asking to quit his post in July, 1973.
>
> But three months shy of his departure, the Police Commissioner received a tip. Police contacted 480 banks and found millions of dollars in overseas and local bank accounts—all controlled by Godber. Once hailed a hero during the 1967 riots for confronting violent protestors, Godber panicked. He asked that his retirement start in June.

> The prospect that he might flee sparked the creation of one of the world's most powerful anti-graft organisations—the Independent Commission Against Corruption.
>
> Events unfolded subsequently at a rapid pace. After eight months of legal battles, the once clean-cut Godber—by then sporting a bushy beard—was extradited to Hong Kong. He was charged with one count of conspiracy and one of bribery, after being accused of taking HK$25,000 from a Chinese Police Superintendent who had been desperate for a promotion. Despite a mountain of evidence amassed over many years, just one witness testified against him. Yet Godber was found guilty in 1976 and sentenced to four years in prison.

The governor set up a committee of enquiry to suggest reforms after the above events. Based on the recommendations of the committee, the Independent Commission Against Corruption (ICAC) was set up in 1974 under an Ordinance and replaced the Police Department's Anti-corruption Unit. The eradication of corruption through ICAC, however, had a difficult beginning. Initially, the ICAC investigators and police had highly adversarial relations. These reached a flash point when in 1977 following the successful smashing of drug racket by ICAC, which was operating from a fruit market, the police stormed the ICAC headquarters. The Governor then decided to grant pardon for past offences and start a new chapter. However, cases which were deemed very serious were to be pursued. The police felt that it gave them a fresh chance to reform.

The Commission is now answerable directly to the Chief Executive of the Hong Kong Special Administrative Region (earlier the Governor). It has a staff of about 12,100. Its budget in 2012 was $112 million most of which was spent on staff. Of the total strength, 75 per cent were working in operation, 5 per cent in prevention and 20 per cent in community relations—the three divisions which comprised the commission. The Commission has extensive powers of search and seizure, including bank accounts. These include:[16]

(a) examine bank accounts.

(b) require a suspect to produce material for investigation.

(c) obtain information from the Inland Revenue Department.

(d) require a suspect to furnish under a statutory declaration details of assets acquired or disposed of by him or her.

(e) require any other person to furnish information relevant to a suspected Prevention of Bribery Ordinance (POBO) offence under a statutory declaration or on oath.

(f) search premises and seize evidence.

(g) restrain property believed to be proceeds of corruption.

(h) arrest and detain suspects in the Commission's detention centre (for up to 48 hours) following which they must either be charged and brought before court, or released, either on bail or unconditionally.

(i) require a suspect to surrender his or her travel documents pending investigation; and

(j) investigating officers can make arrests relating to these offences.

Two main ordinances which govern the eradication of corruption are ICAC and POBO. The ordinance on bribery has provisions against corruption in private sector. Considering that Hong Kong is a financial centre for international trade, the corruption is punishable both in public and private sectors. Provisions of Section 4 make corruption a punishable offence in public sector for bribe-giver and bribe-taker. Section 9 similarly makes it an offence for such acts in private sector.

The strategy adopted by ICAC to reduce corruption has three parts. First, it investigates complaints of corruption after receipt of such allegations. Second, it examines the practices and procedures of different government offices and suggests changes. Third, it undertakes community relations, informs the public about corruption and educates them against it. These three functions are undertaken in operations, corruption prevention and community relations departments of ICAC. The operation division examines all complaints to find out the truth. It is unlike Singapore, Corruption Prevention and Combating Bureau (CPCB) which selects cases and sends the rest to regular investigating agencies. Based on the results of investigations, prosecution is launched by the Department of Justice which takes the decision on prosecution matters. The Prevention of Corruption Division helps the department in simplifying procedures. It is based on the principle of procedural simplicity, transparency and accountability. While it encourages the departments to undertake reforms themselves and suggests setting up of integrity Steering Committee, it also offers advisory services for formulation of a new legislation, policies and procedures to facilitate public service. It also acts as an adviser to the Civil Service Bureau of the Hong Kong Government. The civil service is required to maintain a code of conduct.

The ICAC inter-community relations strategy undertakes two specific functions:

(a) Educating the public against the evil of corruption.

(b) Enlisting and fostering public support in combating corruption.

In its drive to inculcate education, it addresses issues of integrity in public sector. These efforts include developing code of conduct for officials and introducing ethic officer programme to promote ethical values.

The work of ICAC is monitored by four independent Monitoring Committees. These comprise leading citizens. The four Committees are: Advisory Committee on Corruption, the Operations Review Committee, the Corruption Prevention Advisory Committee and Citizens Advisory Committee on Community Relations.

Hong Kong's success with its anti-corruption efforts is due to several factors. First, it had a strong commitment in the beginning and passed two very tough legislations, the ICAC and POBO. Second, it worked a strategy which laid emphasis on all aspects of corruption, including community education and prevention. Third, quite like Singapore, they set up an independent body away from existing police force. This was a start with no baggage of the past.

Political Corruption in Some National Economies

Petty corruption in major developed economies is not very significant. However, it is the large political corruption which has plagued almost all nations. Ackerman (1999: 28-30) gives examples of the very wide and extensive nature of grand corruption or political corruption in several economies of the world including New Zealand, Paraguay, Indonesia, Zimbabwe, South Korea, Italy, Germany and France.[17] To understand the causes underlying such corruption, we consider some instances of these types of corruption in the US, Italy, and Brazil.

There have been a number of instances of corrupt behaviour by very senior politicians in the US. One of the earliest cases of corruption started with William M. Tweed who was elected to the House of Representatives in 1852 and subsequently in New York City Board of Advisors and to New York State Senate. Tweed was convicted in 1873 for his role in corruption and given a 12-year sentence. Governor of Tennessee in 1975 was accused of extortion, conspiracy to sell pardons, paroles and commutations by FBI and convicted. Budd Dwyer, a member of the House of Representatives (1955–1970), was later charged with campaign donations from a computer company for a quid pro quo exchange of $4 million contract. He was also charged with mail fraud, inter-state transportation in aiding racketeering and conspiracy to commit bribing. He was sentenced to 55 years in prison and $300,000 fine. Edwin Edwards (1972-1996) served as Governor of Louisiana for four terms and later charged by FBI for involvement in extortion from businessmen and benefits in return for river Casino Licences. In 1998, he was convicted and found guilty of extortion, fraud, racketeering and conspiracy. He was 80 years then and sought pardon from President Bush. Spiro Agnew served as Vice President of the US under President Richard Nixon (1969-1973). Later he was charged with accepting bribes worth more than $100,000 in his earlier political career in Maryland and also investigated for tax fraud, extortion and conspiracy. Later it was revealed in a Civil Court that he had in fact accepted a sum of $147,000 as bribes while working as Governor of Maryland. He was later found to reimburse a cash amount of $268,000. Caroll Hubbard was a member of the House of Representatives, six times before being defeated in 1992 primary. He was indicted for misuse of government property and personnel (1992). In 1990s, he was convicted of violating federal campaign spending rules, theft and obstruction of Justice. He was sentenced for three years in Federal Prison and fined $150,000 (approx.). Ryan served as

Governor of Illinois (1999-2003) and later in 2006, he was found guilty of racketeering, bribery, money laundering, extortion and for fraud. He was sentenced to six and a half years in prison. Cunningham was a member of the US House in 1991-2005. Later he sat on House Sub-Committee that designates spending to certain defence programmes. He pleaded guilty to accepting bribes of $2.4 million from at least three defense contractors in exchange for government business. In 2006, he was sentenced to eight years in prison and ordered to pay a fine of $1.8 million.[18]

The Lockheed affair was a case involving bribes in several countries. Officials of the US aerospace company, Lockheed were found to have paid bribes of $22 million to foreign officials.[19] The allegations were made against West German Minister for Defense. Similar allegations were also made against Minister, Prime Minister and President of Italy. There were also charges of corruption against office of Japanese Prime Minster Kakei Tanaka that bribes of $3 million were paid to them to influence their buying of L-1011 instead of Douglas DC-10 by All Nippon Airways (ANA). Tanaka was arrested in 1976 and later sentenced to four years imprisonment in October 1983.[20] It was also alleged that Prince Bernhard of Netherlands had also received a bribe of $1.1 million from Lockheed to ensure that Lockheed-104 would win over Mirage-5 for purchase contract. After an enquiry by Prime Minister Joop den Uyl of Netherlands, a constitutional crisis ensued and it was reported that Queen Juliana threatened to abdicate if Bernhard was prosecuted. He was consequently spared but forbidden to wear his army uniform.[21]

This widespread corruption due to Lockheed's desire to win international contracts led to resignation of Chairman and Vice Chairman of the company from its board. It also led to debates in the US. In the light of the above experience, the US later passed a law against corruption in procuring foreign contracts.

Selvio Berlusconi, the former Prime Minister of Italy for varying periods during 1994-2011, was accused of giving € 3 million bribe to the then Senator Sergio De Gregorio to entice him to defect and join Berlusconi's party.[22] After De Gregorio demitted office as a Senator, he admitted to bribe and was sentenced to 20-months prison sentence. He was also convicted for tax fraud and four years in jail. Massimo Maria Berruti, an MP from Forza Italia, was sentenced to eight months for aiding and abetting in a trial for bribes. Vito Bonsignore, European MP, was sentenced to two years for attempted corruption in the construction of a hospital. Umberto Bossi, former Minister for Federal Reforms, was sentenced to eight months for Enmont bribe. Gianstefano Frigerio, MP for Forza Italia, was sentenced for three years and nine months on grounds of corruption. One of the widely discussed cases of corruption was of Enmont deal of the 1990s. By one estimate, it might have generated $289 million in kickbacks and bribes.

Amongst the developing countries, Brazil has a history of large-scale political corruption, though it has high per capita income of $11,204. On Corruption Perceptions Index (CPI) scale it is placed at 72nd rank in 2013. While this did not indicate very high level of corruption, according to the study by Federation of Industry of South Paulo State (FIESPS), the total average annual estimate of corruption in Brazil was 1.38-2.3% of GDP (gross domestic product).[23] Clearly, corruption levels were high. We give one instance of such political corruption. Two reports in *Economist* on 15th and 23rd November, 2013 pointed out the weakness in the Brazilian law which allowed 25 politicians and businessmen convicted of Menselao (or big monthly stipend) to stay out of jail even in 2013, though the scandal was known in 2005. They were found guilty of bribing, money laundering and corruption. The sentences in some cases were more than eight years which made them ineligible for, under Brazilian law, of lenient treatment or soft handling like house arrest or community service. Four of the above were able to hold seat in the Congress, in spite of the above conviction by Supreme Court. The report mentioned that finally Supreme Court in a surprise move dismissed their appeals and issued warrants for the arrest of Jose Dirceu and 11 others. As a result, Dirceu went to jail along with other prominent politicians. The nature of the corruption in the above case was extremely outrageous, as the report of the *Economist* pointed out on 23 November 2013:

> As many Brazilians are still watching incredulously the imprisonment of the principal figures in the Mensel ao (big monthly payments) scandal, the scheme in which public funds were used to buy political support for the then Lula da Silva government and to pay off deals from the election campaign...

According to investigations carried out by Federal Police and Brazilian Court of Audit, the amount in cash-for-votes was $43 million of tax-payers' money. The softness of the treatment of Brazilian legal system is an incentive for political corruption.

Global experience has several lessons on corruption. First, petty corruption may be reduced very significantly, but the political corruption and grand corruption is very difficult to manage and reduce. Second, countries with records of success in minimising corruption fall in two categories: those with very high level of political commitment like Hong Kong and Singapore and those whose societies are traditionally egalitarian and also have a very high level of per capita incomes like Finland, Denmark and other Nordic countries. Third, strong laws on conflict of interest, political party financing and transparency of senior public officials with a strong monitoring mechanism to ensure implementation and quick investigation and punishment irrespective of the rank can provide a strong bulwark against corruption. Fourth, corruption fighting strategy must include strategy for rapid economic growth leading to improved standards of living, measures for prevention of corruption, education on corruption and quick and fair investigation with fast track prosecution of the accused.

Notes and References

1. Meagher, P. (2004). "'Anti-corruption Agencies: A Review of Experience", *Discussion Papers on Institutions and Development* No. 04/02. Maryland: Center for Institutional Reform and the Informal Sector (IRIS Center), University of Maryland.
2. Ibid.
3. Transparency International (TI) has published the Corruption Perceptions Index (CPI) annually ranking countries "by their perceived levels of corruption, as determined by expert assessments and opinion surveys." The CPI generally defines corruption as "the misuse of public power for private benefits". CPI for the year 2013 is available at: *http://cpi.transparency.org/cpi2013* (accessed on 20 July 2014).
4. The primary World Bank collection of development indicators, compiled from officially recognised international sources. It presents the most current and accurate global development data available, and includes national, regional and global estimates. It is available at: *http://data.worldbank.org/about/world-development-indicators-data* (accessed on 20 July 2014).
5. European Commission's Anti-Corruption Report (2014). Brussels, 3.2.2014 COM (2014) 38, Annex 26. It's available at: *http://formin.finland.fi/public/download.aspx?ID=100254&GUID=%7B4E90D9A4-B5EE-4EB9-B823-CCA228632695%7D* (accessed on 29 August 2014).
6. OECD Publication on "Public Sector Integrity: A Framework for Assessment". It's available at: *http://www.integriteitoverheid.nl/fileadmin/BIOS/data/Publicaties/Downloads/OECD_Publication_Public_Sector_Integrity_-_a_framework_for_assesment.pdf* (accessed on 29 August 2014).
7. Gini index measures the extent to which the distribution of income or consumption expenditure among individuals or households within an economy deviates from a perfectly equal distribution. A Lorenz curve plots the cumulative percentages of total income received against the cumulative number of recipients, starting with the poorest individual or household. The Gini index measures the area between the Lorenz curve and a hypothetical line of absolute equality, expressed as a percentage of the maximum area under the line. Thus a Gini index of 0 represents perfect equality, while an index of 1 implies perfect inequality.
8. Ease of doing business ranks economies from 1 to 189, with first place being the best. A high ranking (a low numerical rank) means that the regulatory environment is conducive to business operation. The index averages the country's percentile rankings on 10 topics covered in the World Bank's Doing Business. The ranking on each topic is the simple average of the percentile rankings on its component indicators.
9. The Hobbs Act was passed in 1946 as an amendment to the 1934 Anti-Racketeering Act. Both laws target labour racketeering and organised crime activities, but the Hobbs Act has been used successfully in recent years against armed robbers who victimise businesses. The law criminalises obstruction, delay, or impact on interstate commerce by robbery or extortion with the use of actual or threatened violence. Benefits of the Hobbs Act; there are three main advantages: (a) The penalties are harsher than in local prosecutions. Sentences of 20, 30 or 50 years, and even life sentences, have already been handed out by federal courts around the country; (b) Since the federal system has no parole, anyone receiving a federal sentence serves out the full term (no early out for good behaviour); and (c) Faced with long prison sentences, some of the suspects in these cases will cooperate with law enforcement and prosecutors—giving up names and knowledge of other crimes—in return for reduced sentences. The Travel Act, 18 U.S.C. §1952, is a Federal criminal statute which forbids the use of the US mail, or interstate or foreign travel, for the purpose of engaging in certain specified criminal acts. It was first passed by United States Congress in 1961 and

has been amended six times since then. Racketeer Influenced and Corrupt Organizations Act, commonly referred to as the RICO Act or simply RICO, is a US federal law that provides for extended criminal penalties and a civil cause of action for acts performed as part of an ongoing criminal organisation. The RICO Act focuses specifically on racketeering and it allows the leaders of a syndicate to be tried for the crimes which they ordered others to do or assisted them, closing a perceived loophole that allowed someone who told a man to, for example, murder, to be exempt from the trial because he did not actually commit the crime personally. RICO was enacted by section 901(a) of the Organized Crime Control Act of 1970. The first mail fraud legislation was adopted in 1872. As part of a general revision of the postal laws, Congress made it a crime to mail material intended to effectuate "any scheme or artifice to defraud" [an act to revise, consolidate and amend the statutes relating to the Post Office Department, ch. 335, § 301, 17 Stat. 283, 323 (1872) (repealed)]. This provision evoked almost no discussion in Congress, so there is little legislative history to provide guidance to the courts.

10. The Foreign Corrupt Practices Act (FCPA), enacted in 1977, generally prohibits the payment of bribes to foreign officials to assist in obtaining or retaining business. The FCPA can apply to prohibited conduct anywhere in the world and extends to publicly traded companies and their officers, directors, employees, stockholders and agents. Agents can include third party agents, consultants, distributors, joint venture partners and others; theft or bribery concerning programmes receiving Federal funds (sometimes referred to as programme fraud or programme bribery) is a Federal crime under 18 U.S.C. §666. The purpose of this statute is to protect the integrity of the vast sums of money distributed through Federal programmes. The section is designed to facilitate the prosecution of persons who steal money or otherwise divert property or services from state and local governments or private organisations—for example, universities, foundations and business corporations—that receive large amounts of Federal funds.

11. The FCPA of 1977 is a US Federal law known primarily for two of its main provisions, one that addresses accounting transparency requirements under the Securities Exchange Act of 1934 and another concerning bribery of foreign officials.

12. The Ethics in Government Act of 1978 is a US Federal law that was passed in the wake of the Nixon watergate scandal and the Saturday night massacre. It created mandatory, public disclosure of financial and employment history of public officials and their immediate family. It also created restrictions on lobbying efforts by public officials for a set period after leaving public office. Last, it created the US Office of Independent Counsel, tasked with investigating government officials.

13. Quah, Jon S.T. (1999). "Corruption in Asian Countries: Can it be Minimized?" in *Public Administration Review* 59(6).

14. The Prevention of Corruption Act (PCA) was enacted in June 1960 to provide for the more effectual prevention of corruption. The law also empowers CPIB officers to investigate and arrest corrupt offenders. The PCA was amended a few times since its enactment. Through these amendments, punishments for corrupt offenders were enhanced and CPIB officers were given more investigative powers to make the fight against corruption easier. Details are available at: *http://app.cpib.gov.sg/cpib_new/user/default.aspx?pgID=201*.

15. *http://www.nytimes.com/2007/04/09/world/asia/09iht-sing.3.5200498.html* (accessed on 29 Aug, 2014).

16. *http://www.scmp.com/news/hong-kong/article/1428093/forty-years-its-creation-how-icac-cleaned-corruption-hong-kong?page=all* (accessed on 29 Aug, 2014).

17. Hong Kong was in a state of rapid change in the 1960s and 1970s. The massive growth in population and fast expansion of the manufacturing industry accelerated the pace of social and economic development. The government, while maintaining social order and delivering

the bare essentials in housing and other services, was unable to meet the insatiable needs of the swelling population. This provided a fertile environment for the unscrupulous. Many people had to take the 'backdoor route' simply to earn a living and secure other than basic services. 'Tea money', 'black money', 'hell money'—whatever its name—became not only familiar to many Hong Kong people, but accepted with resignation as a necessary way of life. Since its inception in 1974, the Independent Commission Against Corruption has embraced a three-pronged approach of law enforcement, prevention and community education to fight corruption. With the support of the government and the community, Hong Kong has now become one of the cleanest places in the world. Details available at: *http://www.icac.org.hk/en/about_icac/bh/*

18. Ackerman, Susan R. (1999). *Corruption and Government: Causes Consequences and Reforms.* Cambridge University Press.
19. Grossman, Mark (2003). *Political Corruption in America: An Encyclopedia of Scandals, Power and Greed, Political Corruption in America: An Encyclopedia of Scandals, Power, and Greed.* Vol. 1. Grey House Publishing. See also: Clark, K. (1996). "Do We Have Enough Ethics in Governance Yet? An Answer from Fiduciary Theory", *U. ILL. L. REV.* 57; Crain, Andrew D. (2014). *The Ford Presidency: A History.* McFarland Publishers.
20. "Lockheed Agrees to Pay Record Fine : Aerospace—Calabasas Firm Pleads Guilty in Connection with Bribing an Egyptian politician", *Los Angeles Times*. Details available at *http://articles.latimes.com/1995-01-28/business/fi-25231_1_egyptian-politician* (Accessed on 23 April 2013); See also: Rich, Ben R. and Leo Janos (1994). *Skunk Works: A Personal Memoir of My Years at Lockheed.* New York: Little Brown & Co.p.10.
21. Hunziker, S. and I. Kamimura (1996). *Kakuei Tanaka: A Political Biography of Modern Japan.* Cavendish Square Publishing.
22. Hartung., William D. (2010). *Prophets of War: Lockheed Martin and the Making of Military-Industrial Complex.* Nation Books.
23. *http://www.telegraph.co.uk/news/worldnews/europe/italy/10630286/Silvio-Berlusconi-goes-on-trial-over-2.5m-bribe-to-opposition-defector.html* (accessed on 29 August 2014).
24. *http://www.forbes.com/fdc/welcome_mjx.shtml* (accessed on 29 August 2014).

Annexure Table A-4.1

Anti-Corruption Agency (ACA) Powers

	Select Cases	*Investigate Abuses in Public Sector*	*Investigate Abuses in Private Sector*	*Make Arrests*	*Search and Seizure*	*Conduct Surveillance Operations*	*Prosecute*
NSW Australia (ICAC)	Yes	Yes	Yes	Yes	Yes		No
Botswana (DCEC)	No	Yes	Yes	Yes	Yes		No
Ecuador (CCCC)		Yes	No				
Hong Kong (ICAC)	No	Yes	Yes	Yes	Yes	Yes	No
India (CVC)		Yes					No
Singapore (CPIB)	No	Yes	Yes	Yes	Yes	Yes	No
Thailand (NCCC)		Yes		Yes	Yes		
Uganda (Inspectorate)		Yes		Yes			No
Argentina (ACO)	Yes	Yes					No
Malaysia (ACA)	No	Yes	Yes	Yes	Yes	Yes	No
Tanzania (PCB)	Yes	Yes					No
Philippines (Ombudsman)		Yes					Yes
US (OGE)				No	No	No	No
France (SCPC)		Yes	Yes				No

Annexure Table A-4.2

Independence of Anti-Corruption Agencies in Different Countries

	Who Appointment Chair?	*Term of Chair*	*To Whom Agency Reports?*	*Are Reports Public?*	*Own Line in Budget?*
NSW Australia	Governor	Up to 5 years	NSW Parliament	Yes	Yes
Botswana (DCEC)	President	President's discretion	President	Yes	
Ecuador (CCCC)	Elected by Commission			Yes	Yes
Hong Kong (ICAC)	Governor		Governor	Yes	Yes
India (CVC)	President	3 years	Parliament	Yes	
Singapore (CPIB)	President	President's discretion	Prime Minister	No	No
Thailand (NCCC)	Elected by Commission		Senate		Yes
Uganda (Inspectorate)	President	4 years, renewable once	Parliament		Yes
Argentina (ACO)	President		President	Yes	No
Malaysia (ACA)	King, on PM's recommendation	Usually 2 years, renewable	Prime Minister	Yes	No
Tanzania (PCB)	President	President's direction	President/ Chief Sec. of House	Yes	No
Philippines (Ombudsman)	President	7 years; renewable	President/ Congress	Yes	Yes
US (OGE)	President	5 years		Yes	Yes
France (SCPC)			MOJ/PM		No

5

Fighting Corruption with Economic Growth

The strategies for fighting corruption by different countries have generally focused on regulatory measures. This is primarily due to the fact that corruption is considered a social evil which needs to be uprooted with administrative measures. A number of countries have passed laws defining corruption and set up anti-corruption agencies to catch corrupt people. This approach has been generally considered quite adequate to address the issues of corruption in the past. In recent years, there has been a fresh thinking on these policies. The experience of Hong Kong based on a more comprehensive approach, which was in several areas similar to that of Singapore, has been generally considered more appropriate for addressing the menace of corruption. It has, however, limitations since both the experiences are for comparatively small populations. The solutions which have been given by these countries, therefore, when applied to major global economies like India, China or the US which have large multi-cultural societies with huge geographical area and large number of local bodies, with institutions which have different organisational culture, have only a limited application. We suggest an alternate strategy to fight corruption centred around economic growth.

Income and Corruption

Sociologists, civil servants and political administrators have not adequately realised importance of the ecosystem which is necessary for addressing the problem of corruption. The experience of the global economies as mentioned in our earlier chapters is that corruption is strongly correlated with per capita incomes when all economies are considered together. Such level of incomes require rapid economic growth. We study the relationship between incomes and corruption to find how increased incomes can be a major instrument in fighting corruption and limitations of this policy.

Figure 5.1

Average Corruption Index versus GDP Per Capita Slabs

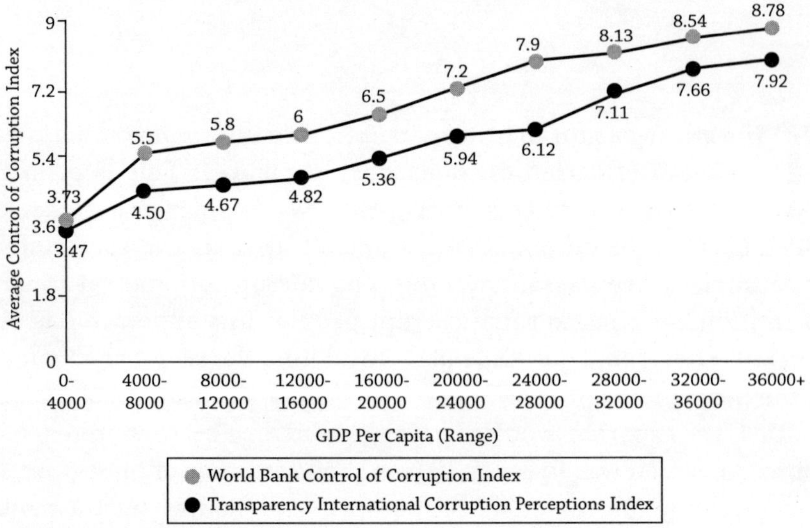

While considering impact of income on corruption, we have already considered the results of regression analysis. Our analysis shows that increase in income lowers corruption and a sharp change takes place in the ability of per capita incomes to lower corruption at \$4,000-\$5,000 (Figure 5.1). At these incomes, corruption level starts declining. We now consider the relationship to find whether low incomes by themselves also act as a constraint for lowering corruption. We use an alternate method to find this. We consider Corruption Perceptions Index (CPI) of the Transparency International (TI) in countries of different income groups. For this, we use the World Bank criterion of segregating world economies into four major income groups based on GNI (gross national income) per capita: low income, lower middle income, upper middle income and high income.[1] We have used this classification in earlier chapters too.

We find that there is not a single country in the world lying either in low income, lower middle income or upper middle income group (i.e., GNI per capita less than or equal to $12,615) which has very low level of corruption (corruption index greater than 7.0). Of the low income countries, 54.8 per cent have extremely high levels of corruption with CPI less than 3.0, and 42.0 per cent of the countries of this group have slightly lower but still fairly large levels of corruption with CPI in the range of 3.0-5.0. In lower middle income countries, share of countries with extremely high levels of corruption with CPI less than 3.0 declines to 40.0 per cent and of those with lower corruption with 3.0-5.0 CPI increases to 54.3 per cent. There is also an increase in share of countries with medium level of corruption with CPI in the range of 5.0-7.0 to 5.7 per cent from 3.2 per cent. A clear shift is noticeable in corruption level of countries with transition from low income to lower middle income group. This trend continues in the next two income groups too. In upper middle income group, the share of countries with CPI less than 3.0 further declines to 17.1 per cent and then to 4.25 per cent in high income group. Also, the share of countries with CPI in 3.0-5.0 range increases to 65.7 per cent from 54.3 per cent and 42.0 per cent respectively of earlier groups. The share of countries with lower level of corruption goes on increasing in higher income groups. In the high income group, 46.8 per cent of the countries have CPI more than 7.0 indicating a very high proportion of very low corruption countries at high income levels[2] (Annexure Table A-5.3).

The analysis indicates that the level of corruption in different income groups as indicated by average level of corruption index keeps on reducing with increased incomes. The percentage of lower corruption countries in each group increases with each higher income group. The most significant feature is the existence of boundary condition. It operates in each income group and indicates the limit beyond which either the country of that group cannot reduce corruption level or may be able to reduce only in very few cases. While different countries of the group may have different corruption levels, it is not possible for them to cross the boundary so long as they are part of that income group. For countries of low and lower middle income, this is operative at CPI level of 5.0 and in very rare cases at 7.0; in upper middle income, this is at 7.0 and increases to 10.0 CPI in high income country group. Clearly low incomes act as a constraint on lowering corruption.

Increase in incomes makes an impact on the governance system too. With economic growth, new institutions and principles of governance and reforms are in evidence in varying degrees in different countries. The process of growth necessitates new investments and improved efficiency. This improves the ecosystem for overall governance. Different countries try to build on this in different ways. The corruption levels come down based on efforts made by the governments. However, these policy interventions are more successful if incomes are high. At income levels of less than $4,000-$5,000, the corrupt behaviour is strong; a major improvement in governance is required to reduce corruption. Most countries find it difficult to do so. In spite of best efforts, the countries are not able to reduce corruption further. The low incomes act as a pull down factor on the efficacy of governance reforms. This pull down factor reduces in intensity as incomes go beyond the above critical income levels. With reduced level of pull at higher incomes, the governance reforms are more effective in lowering corruption. In spite of the pull factor, it is however possible for low income countries to reduce corruption up to the boundary of each income group with strong policy reforms.

Drag Effect

The above approach clearly emphasises the need to step-up growth to increase incomes. The problem with this policy is that high economic growth in the face of high corruption may be difficult to achieve. This reduces its efficacy. We look at global experience to ascertain whether the impact of corruption reduces overall growth very sharply or acts merely as a drag, and reasonable GDP growth is still possible. The extent of impact on corruption has been considered by several authors. According to them, one index point increase in corruption reduces growth by 0.1 to 0.5 per cent annually.[3] The reduction in rates of growth, if corruption were to be removed completely, is estimated at about 2.0 per cent. It has not been possible even for some of the most developed economies to completely eliminate corruption. We have no country which has zero corruption. The loss of growth due to corruption has to be benchmarked to average of global corruption level or that of Organisation for Economic Co-operation and Development (OECD) countries. The loss in GDP growth in such a case is about 1.00-1.25 per cent. This is still a large negative impact on annual growth. The average growth in global economies during 1996-2012, in spite of the above drag, was 4.12 per cent and in low income economies was about 4.00 per cent. India recorded a growth of 6.9 per cent during this period. There were a number of countries which recorded low or very marginal growth in this period. This growth was possible in spite of high level of global corruption. It can further accelerate if countries can reform their economic policies and economic institutions. In all such countries, corruption will no doubt continue to be a millstone slowing down progress. However, the argument that growth will just not be possible unless corruption goes down is not true. Countries can increase their economic growth though at reduced levels. On a sustained basis, if the growth continues for long periods, it will help create an ecosystem, due to increased incomes, which is far better suited for reducing corruption and drag effect will keep on reducing. A recent study using empirical assessment shows that economic growth leads to lower corruption. After a study of 13,000 Vietnamese firms, it makes the following observation:[4]

> We show that economic growth is predicted to decrease the rate of bribe extraction under plausible assumptions, with the benefit to officials of demanding a given share of revenue as bribes outweighed by the increased risk that firms will move elsewhere. This effect is dampened if firms are less mobile. We find, first, that firm growth indeed causes a decrease in bribe extraction. Second, this pattern is particularly true for firms with strong land rights and those with operations in multiple provinces, consistent with these firms being more mobile. Our results suggest that as poor countries grow, corruption could subside "on its own".

While corruption may not subside of its own, growth in incomes has a strong positive effect.

We now look at some limitation to the increase in growth approach. We look at impact of per capita incomes through several transmission channels to fully understand the nature of this relationship. We identify four areas: civil service, investment, government expenditure, expanding middle class and media.

Civil Service

In most economies with low incomes, the civil service is not very well paid.[5] Many of them, therefore, use the opportunity which they get during the course of their work to create hurdles and extract money from whichever position they enjoy. In many cases, their aspirations are fairly high and there is a huge gap between their requirements based on these aspirations and the wages which they get from the government. This leads to major corruption in the system. When income levels rise sufficiently, there is a corresponding increase in the emoluments of civil servants. This leads to lower requirements or needs which they seek to meet from other sources. The reduced gap between aspirations and their salary structure has a positive impact. It leads to reduced level of corruption. This impact is noticeable only at high per capita incomes. In low income economies, the countries are not able to make major upward revision in salary structure due to poor financial resources and competing priorities. Countries like Singapore made very large increase in the salary structure of their civil servants and ministers. It has enabled it to develop a very clean society.[6]

Investment

Increase in per capita income requires larger investment and higher efficiency. Since governance is weak in most of the developing economies, higher incomes are primarily driven by higher investment. In economies with high level of corruption, this provides an opportunity for collecting bribes. It also helps improve governance as we see later. Many of these economies had large investments in the last 15 years. There share in the overall investments have increased as against OECD economies. According to International Monetary Fund (IMF), investment in non-OECD countries during 1996-2012 was 24 per of the world's total investment. In absolute terms, the total investments in these economies increased to $8.67 trillion in 2012 as against $1.55 trillion in 1996. High rates of savings in China, India,

Indonesia, Malaysia and Singapore have fuelled growth rates in several major economies of Asia including some of these.

We look at various areas of investment to assess different ways in which investment can help reduce corruption and help development of new institutions. One of the areas where large investments take place is infrastructure. To increase growth rates, it is now a well-accepted view that a good infrastructure is essential. Developing economies have shortage of public resources. They like to attract private investment. In many areas, such investment is not financially viable. Take for example construction of roads. It is not a profitable investment unless tolls can be charged from users of the roads. Countries have developed PPP (public-private partnership) contract models. These require development of documents defining terms of concession of the private investor who constructs and maintains the road. To make his investment profitable, he is permitted to charge toll from users of the road. The concession is for an agreed period after which the road reverts back to state government or local authority. Many countries use the global best practices to finalise these terms. This results in creation of new institutions where transparency is strongly emphasised. Often this involves intermediation of international institutions and their procedures and agreements are accepted. The incorporation of principles of conflict of interest, accountability of government, and standards of performance monitored by independent engineers are concepts used in several of these agreements. These principles can be used in most government sectors. This helps in improvement of governance as people apply these to wider government functioning.

Another example can be the investments made by private industry in an area. There is a lot of corruption at grass-roots level. States or local bodies compete with each other to make the system simpler and attract investment. The World Bank has classified countries according to ease of doing business.[7] The inputs from better performing countries are used by many states in India to improve procedures, change regulations and laws. These help evolving of improved systems, which are less prone to corruption.

We can look at another illustration. The number of private players in the economies has increased rapidly. Many of them are providing services to general public. A number of regulatory institutions have developed as a result of this. These prescribe rules for the functioning of these players. All these have been necessitated primarily due to private investment. The investments in the economy require clear policies on repatriation of profits, tax laws which need to be simple, foreign investments, and foreign exchange laws and regulations in different sectors about raising debt from international markets. Large expansion of the economy has led to rules prescribing greater transparency in maintenance of accounts and auditing. For private sector investments, the government may prescribe standards of service and accountability especially for service industry. These concepts are applicable to several sectors and citizens may often insist on it. The governance improves with greater transparency, accountability and other principles of good governance. This lowers corruption levels.

We now look at how investment can have negative effect and result in increased corruption. There is a strong belief that the economic reforms in India, in the 1990s, led to higher level of investment and corruption. In the last few years, Comptroller and Auditor General of India (CAG)[8] gave a number of reports criticising government policies on natural resource allocation, especially spectrum allocation and coal block allocation. These reports have given further credence to this view. In countries with high level of corruption, as the size of investment goes up, new opportunities are perceived by civil servants and politicians to extract bribes. Investment in these countries in the last 15 years has increased sharply as evidenced by fast growth of GDP. The GDP of India has gone up by 4 times and of China by nearly 10 times during 1996-2012. The GDP of a large number of other developing economies has also increased rapidly during this period. Indonesia's GDP went up 4 times, Brazil's by 3 times and in Malaysia it increased by 3 times. The increase in GDP has been possible due to increased investments and better efficiency of the economies. The larger size of the economies in many countries and higher investment by more than five and a half times in terms of money in non-OECD economies have provided large potential for corruption. The very rapid increase in GDP and investment is bound to result in higher corruption in absolute money terms in countries with poor governance. It is possible that even in terms of the size of economy, these countries have higher corruption. In other countries, with better governance institutions, it may be lower. The economic expansion in recent years has happened at a faster rate in developing economies. Countries like China and India have recorded growths of 10 per cent and 6.9 per cent respectively in the last two decades. The standards of governance being poor in many of these countries, higher investment could result in higher corruption at least in money terms. Level of corruption being already high in many of these countries, the belief that corruption has increased in recent years would have a strong basis.

Some of the views in public discourse are driven by perception of people. They see around themselves several corrupt individuals with demand for larger bribes for clearing investments or providing services. The number of public servants and their agents demanding money are also more numerous. The expansion of the economy in new areas of services and IT (information technology) has created a new class of agents engaged in collecting bribes. In India, one sees this in environment, mining, telecom, power and other infrastructure sectors. It is exhibited in delivery of plan funds and of public services. Globally it is manifest in international trade, defence purchases and various oil exploration concessions.

We find that investments in the global economies have multiplied several times and money value of corruption has also simultaneously gone up. It appears that existing measurement does not capture fully the political corruption in these investments. Larger investments have also given clear benefits in terms of development of better governance practices and higher income levels. The evolution of new institutions, principles and laws incorporating procedures and safeguards makes it difficult for corruption to expand, and helps improve governance. Growth process will necessarily need larger investments in the economy. There are two clearly opposite impacts of the investments especially in poorly governed societies. We can reconcile the two and work on a clear strategy to lower corruption. Until incomes by themselves increase adequately and act as a major bulwark against corruption, countries should focus on improving governance using some of the principles and concepts involved in investment and other supportive ideas. This will help lower corruption and continued growth.

Government Expenditure

Per capita income increase enables higher tax realisation and larger revenues with the governments. These can be used for development purposes. Regression analysis indicates that increase in government expenditure lowers corruption level. There is a strong focus in most of the developing economies on development of education and health as resource availability improves. Universalisation of primary education is a programme which is implemented by all countries. Increased incomes provide an opportunity to expand initiatives in primary and secondary education. While governments have to prioritise expenditure, highest priority is generally given to education by most governments of developing countries. Expansion of education helps reduction of corruption as seen by us earlier. In our analysis, we find that if more than 80 per cent of the population in target age group is enrolled for secondary education, the impact on lowering of corruption is quite manifest. It helps in larger focus on governance by the people.

Both income inequality and high poverty ratio are strong incentives for corrupt behaviour in any society. With larger financial resources available with government, it is possible to provide money for reducing the hardship to such families that have very low income. The experiences of India, Brazil and Mexico indicates some of these possibilities.[9] In countries with very low incomes, such a programme may not be possible as the resources required may be difficult to raise.

Expanding Middle Class and Media

The impact of increased incomes in many democratic societies has in recent years been manifest through larger public awareness and discourse on television, newspapers, social media, internet and civil society. The expansion of middle class also takes place with rising incomes. Both of these outcomes greatly influence good governance and oppose corrupt behaviour. It is quite likely that many of these persons may be engaging in corrupt acts in their functioning. But as a class, they wish to appear opposed to all corrupt acts and champions of moral values. This public posturing greatly influences development of new institutions of governance and reforms of existing institutions. While the economic institutions have an important role, development of political institutions is an important factor in reducing corruption. In many countries where democracy is not well-developed, it is important that the institutions of parliament, the judiciary, the executive, the chief auditor, the election commissioner and the local body institutions are strengthened. In addition, development of a vibrant mechanism which keeps a check over these institutions is another critical factor. In most countries, development of good quality local governments can help reduce corruption to a very great extent for grass-roots delivery of services. A very critical institution in most of the high corruption countries is police. Reforms in police to develop an independent and efficient force with low level of corruption are important. Hong Kong had to develop an alternative mechanism of ICAC to deal with corruption in police. These political and administrative institutions need to be strengthened, made independent, citizen-friendly and accountable. The development of good quality political institutions is a key factor for low corruption. It is these institutions which promote the rule of law on which corruption depends in the society as seen in the earlier chapter. The development of middle class and other outcomes of increased incomes referred to earlier support such changes.

The activism of the civil society can also lead to evolution of people's movement especially if the corruption level is high. Such movements could be in the nature of anti-corruption movement as happened in Delhi.[10] It could also take the form of protests as happened in Hong Kong. These could be supported by media campaign against corruption. Such protests generally result in some reforms in governance system or enactment of new laws. Right to Information (RTI) act, which has provided citizens with right to get information on functioning of government institutions, has been a major instrument in identifying corrupt acts of public servants. This act was a result of public pressure to improve transparency and reduce corruption. Use of information technology in states in India for delivery of public services has expanded as corruption has become a major public issue due to strong public pressure.

The Best and the Worst

While incomes do appear to play a role in reducing corruption, we looked at the experience of global economies in the last 15 years to know the nature of evidence available to support this view. We therefore looked at changes in corruption levels in last 15 years in selected economies. We selected 10 best performing and a similar number of worst performing countries to find reasons for their performance relating to corruption levels. In 80 per cent of the best performing countries, income levels had gone up by a higher margin than the global average. In the worst performing countries, the growth in income levels had either declined or grew at a pace slower than the world average in 70 per cent of the countries. Increase in incomes thus provides a good ecosystem in which anti-corruption reforms are more easily accepted.

Economic growth and increased incomes by themselves are not adequate to address issues concerning corruption. Supportive measures are required to bring corruption levels down. The experience of the selected countries brings this out more clearly. In the first category, we look at cases of countries where corruption levels have reduced sharply. Georgia had very high corruption in 1996. It has gone down in last 15 years. During this period per capita income went up to $2,080, a growth of 155 per cent when average global increase was 27.8 per cent. This created an environment for anti-corruption measures. After the 2003 Rose Revolution, stricter enforcement of laws ensured prosecution of senior corrupt officials. Reforms were undertaken specially in police and public sector. Business environment was deregulated and made liberal. This resulted in one of the highest increase of +3.29 in Corruption Perception Index (CPI) or a drop in corruption when comared with other global economies. Another success story was that of Rwanda. It had a very low per capita income which grew by 89 per cent to $390, in above period. This positive development was accompanied by several other initiatives. This included punishing corrupt officials at all levels, strengthening legal and institutional framework and improving government effectiveness. A strong and competent public sector was built and public finance management system reformed. The increased income was accompanied by a large increase in CPI of +3.17. Liberia is another country which reduced corruption during the above period. President Johnson Sirleaf supported a programme which was given largely by donors. He set up an Anti-Corruption Commission, reformed public financial management and promoted transparent budget processes. These measures helped CPI to increase by+2.33, while per capita incomes increased to $275—a growth by four times as it had a very low base. Another interesting case in this category is that of United Arab Emirates (UAE). The country had a very high per capita income of $24,077 in 2012. Countries in this income level have generally a very low level of corruption. UAE, however, had high corruption levels with CPI of 4.83. Income in the country had declined from $45,490 in 1996 to $24,077 in 2012. The income levels were high enough to have a good ecosystem. The country took several measures to ensure that corruption reduced drastically. It is among some of the very low corruption countries of the word today with CPI of 7.35. The country has simplified tax compliance laws and dealt with cases of corruption of public officials in an even-handed and tough manner. There is increasingly larger compliance of UN Convention against Corruption (UNCAC).

In our analysis of performance of different countries, a major assumption is that other factors specially political stability and governance continue to be at same level. If there is a change, mere economic growth may not be able to stop reform movements in any society. It may lead to higher or lower corruption. Recent political instability in Liberia which may result in higher corruption illustrates this point.

The second category of cases is of the countries which did badly in reducing corruption levels and corruption has worsened. Trinidad and Tobago is one of the countries where corruption has increased very substantially during last 15 years. It is no more part of a select group of countries with very low corruption. The main reason for this decline is the emergence of drug crime in a big way. In 2011, emergency was declared to counter drug-related crime. The deterioration in administrative system is clear. There is high level of corruption in police and judiciary. The government policies have reduced economic freedom making it a less attractive destination. Money laundering is freely done. In spite of very high levels of income and growth in per capita income being impressive, the country has not implemented policies attacking corruption. Its current income level of $14,183, which has doubled in the last decade and half, can enable a reasonable quality of life for its citizens. It is clear that societal environment due to increase in income or high per capita income can be an enabling factor, but by itself not adequate, to reduce corruption. Other measures also influence these levels and in several cases determine the overall corruption environment better. A country falling in the same class is South Africa. It had a per capita income of $4,652 in 1996 which increased during last 15 years by 26.5 per cent, which is slightly below the global average of 27.8 per cent. In spite of above, the corruption level worsened during the above period. Major reason was the highly increased level of political corruption. In absence of political will and charges of corruption against the president Jacob Zuma himself, the corruption level deteriorated sharply. The case of Zimbabwe is quite different. In its case, income levels have fallen by 36.3 per cent to $447 per capita in 2012. These incomes are extremely low and an invitation to corruption. This has made the ecosystem worse and there is consequently widespread corruption in the administration. There is lack of political will. The Zimbabwe anti-corruption agency can be referred to as 'toothless bulldog'. The political will is too weak to undertake reforms.

The global experience has several lessons. First, increase in incomes in general provides a good ecosystem which is conducive for reduction of corruption. By itself it is not sufficient to lower corruption levels. Second, it is possible to very sharply reduce corruption in countries with very low incomes of $500 or less with improved governance and a strong will to act against corrupt ministers and very senior civil servants. Third, even with increased incomes or very high incomes, corruption will continue to be high if top politicians of the country like the president or prime minister are corrupt. They represent the political will of the country to fight against corruption. Fourth, even when growth is good and per capita incomes are above $5,000, countries may have no reduction in corruption levels if the police force is affected by drug-related crimes. Also, even when there is very sharp decline in income but it is still quite high, countries can take governance measures and reach very low level of corruption (Annexure Tables A-5.1 and A-5.2).

The menace of corruption has to be fought through a comprehensive strategy. The citizens of a country are very important stakeholders in this process. They can fight it with greater enthusiasm and be a part of campaign against corruption if social conditions are conducive to it. Without their full participation, the results will be very marginal. This participation is better if incomes increase substantially or are already very high. In such cases, other supportive measures on improving educational levels and reducing inequality and poverty improve the ecosystem for other reform measures further. Governments can take other investments and expand the social sector to further improve human development.

When the above measures are taken, several institutional improvements take place as an integral part of it. The reforms of governance system can then bring other reform measures. These may require political and administrative will in several areas. Action may be required against people at very senior positions in administration, police and political executive. A lot of painstaking work is required to simplify procedures. The delay in the judicial system may need to be addressed. These measures need sustained will and people's support. If the initial ecosystem measures are in place, success in governance reforms may be more effective.

Notes and References

1. Each year on 1 July, The World Bank revises the classification of the world's economies based on estimates of GNI per capita for the previous year. The updated GNI per capita estimates are also used as input to the Bank's operational classification of economies, which determine their lending eligibility. As of 1 July 2013, the World Bank income classifications by GNI per capita are as follows: low income: $1,035 or less; lower middle income: $1,036 to $4,085; upper middle income: $4,086 to $12,615; and high income: $12,616 or more.
2. TI publishes the CPI annually ranking countries by their perceived levels of corruption, as determined by expert assessments and opinion surveys.The CPI generally defines corruption

as "the misuse of public power for private benefit." It measures corruption on a scale of 0-10; higher the index, lower the corruption.

3. Mauro, P. (1995). "Corruption and Growth", *Quarterly Journal of Economics* 110(3), 681–712; See also: Dreher, A. and t. Herzfeld (2005). *The Economic Costs of Corruption: A Survey and New Evidence*. Available at SSRN: *http://ssrn.com/abstract=734184 or http://dx.doi.org/10.2139/ssrn.734184;* Gyimah-Brempong, K. (2002). "'Corruption, Economic Growth, and Income Inequality in Africa", *Economics of Governance* 3: 183–209.
4. Bai, J., S. Jayachandran, Edmund J. Malesky and Benjamin A. Olken (2013). "Does Economic Growth Reduce Corruption? Theory and Evidence from Vietnam", *NBER Working Papers* 19483. National Bureau of Economic Research Inc.
5. Chew, David C.E. (1993). "Civil Service Pay in the Asian-Pacific Region", *Asian Pacific Economic Literature* 7(1); See also: Lienert, I. (1998). "Civil Service Reform in Africa: Mixed Results After 10 Years", *Finance and Development* 35(2); World Bank (1999). *The Hashemite Kingdom of Jordan: Public Sector Review.* Report No. 19664-JO. September 22. Social and Economic Development Group, Middle East and North Africa Region.
6. Mauzy, Dinae K. and R.S. Milne (2002). *Singapore Politics Under People Action Party*. London: Routledge Publication.
7. Ease of doing business ranks economies from 1 to 189, with first place being the best. A high ranking (a low numerical rank) means that the regulatory environment is conducive to business operation. The index averages the country's percentile rankings on 10 topics covered in the World Bank's Doing Business. The ranking on each topic is the simple average of the percentile rankings on its component indicators.
8. The CAG of India is an authority, established by the Constitution of India under Chapter V, who audits all receipts and expenditure of the Government of India (GoI) and the state governments, including those of bodies and authorities substantially financed by the government.
9. For example, in Brazil, Bolsa Família is a social welfare programme of the government, part of federal assistance programmes. Bolsa Família provides financial aid to poor Brazilian families; if they have children, families must ensure that the children attend school and are vaccinated. The programme attempts to both reduce short-term poverty by direct cash transfers and fight long-term poverty by increasing human capital among the poor through conditional cash transfers. It also works to give free education to children who cannot afford to go to school to show the importance of education. In Mexico, *Oportunidades* is a government social assistance programme founded in 2002, based on a previous programme called *Progresa* created in 1997. It is designed to target poverty by providing cash payments to families in exchange for regular school attendance, health clinic visits and nutritional support. *Oportunidades* is credited with decreasing poverty and improving health and educational attainment in regions in which it has been deployed.
10. Anna Hazare started an indefinite hunger strike in New Delhi on 5 April 2011 to exert pressure on the Indian government to enact a stringent anti-corruption law, the Lokpal Bill, 2011, as envisaged in the Jan Lokpal Bill, for the institution of an ombudsman with the power to deal with corruption in public places. The fast led to nationwide protests in support. The fast ended on 9 April 2011, a day after the government accepted Hazare's demands. The government issued a gazette notification on the formation of a joint committee, consisting of government and civil society representatives, to draft the legislation.

Annexure Table A-5.1

Ten Best and Ten Worst Performing Countries on Corruption Scale between 1996 and 2012

Country	*Control of Corruption Index*		*Change in Index (2012 CCI-1996 CCI)*	*% Change in GDP per Capita at Constant 2005 USD during 1996-2012*
	1996	*2012*		
Countries witnessing worsening of corruption during 1996-2012				
Trinidad and Tobago	7.01	4.42	-2.59	+100.00
Cota d'Ivoire	5.40	3.19	-2.21	-7.46
Eritrea	5.89	3.70	-2.19	-23.67
Zimbabwe	4.50	2.45	-2.05	-36.30
South Africa	6.52	4.70	-1.82	+26.50
Yemen, Rep.	4.30	2.54	-1.76	+2.40
Fiji	5.89	4.13	-1.76	+12.50
Kuwait	6.43	4.68	-1.75	-5.50
Turkmenistan	4.05	2.32	-1.73	+157.00
Nepal	4.97	3.35	-1.62	+47.00
Countries witness improvement to corruption during 1996-2012				
Georgia	2.22	5.51	3.29	+155.00
Rwanda	3.14	6.31	3.17	+89.00
UAE	4.83	7.35	2.52	-47.00
Liberia	1.52	3.85	2.33	+420.0
Estonia	4.88	6.96	2.08	+124.00
Macedonia,FYR	3.07	5.04	1.97	+42.00
Latvia	3.36	5.31	1.95	+143.00
Crotia	3.36	4.92	1.56	+47.00
Congo, Dem. Republic.	0.89	2.39	1.50	0.00
Serbia	2.94	4.38	1.44	+58.00

Annexure Table A-5.2

Change in GDP Per Capita of 10 Best and 10 Worst Performing Countries on Corruption Scale Between 1996 and 2012

Country	*GDP Per Capita 1996 at Constant 2005 $*	*GDP Per Capita 2012 at Constant 2005 US$*	*Change in % during 1996-2012*
	Best Performing Countries		
Georgia	816	2080	155
Rwanda	206	390	89
UAE	45490	24077	-47
Liberia	53	276	420
Estonia	5325	11904	124
Macedonia	2450	3478	42
Latvia	3469	8425	143
Croatia	7188	10532	47
Congo, Democratic Republic	164	164	0
Serbia	2433	3856	58
	Worst Performing Status		
Trinidad and Tobago	7100	14183	100
Cote d' Ivoire	1032	955	-7.5
Eritrea	262	200	23.7
Zimbabwe	702	447	-36.3
South Africa	4652	5885	26.5
Yemen	712	729	2.4
Kuwait	31444	29728	-5.5
Turkmenistan	1270	3270	157
Nepal	272	399	47
World	6082	7773	27.8

Annexure Table A-5.3

Percentage of Different Income Group Countries Filling in Various Corruption Slabs

	Corruption Index (0-3.0)		*Corruption Index (3.0-5.0)*		*Corruption Index (5.0-7.0)*		*Corruption Index (7.0+)*	
	WB	*TI*	*WB*	*TI*	*WB*	*TI*	*WB*	*TI*
Low Income Economies	29.0%	54.8%	70.9%	41.9%	0%	3.2%	0%	0%
Lower Middle Income Economies	20.0%	40.0%	77.1%	54.3%	28.5%	5.7%	0%	0%
Upper Middle Income Economies	11.4%	17.1%	60.0%	65.7%	28.6%	17.1%	0%	0%
High Income Economies	2.13%	4.25%	8.50%	17.0%	31.9%	31.9%	57.4%	46.8%

Note: WB = World Bank, TI = Transparency International.

Source: Corruption Index from the World Bank and Transparency International both are on the scale of 0-10.

6

Corruption

The Indian Scene

A Historical Perspective

Corruption has been a part of governance literature in India for more than 2000 years. Chanakya, in his well-celebrated work *Arthashastra*, has given extensive description of how the corrupt officials can be caught, corruption prevented, and the scales of punishment which they deserve. He describes 40 ways in which corrupt officials can work. Following quote from his above work elaborates this:[1]

> What has accrued first is realised afterwards, what is to accrue later is realized first, what is to be carried out is not carried out, what is not to be carried out is carried out, what is carried out is made out as not carried out, what is not carried out is made out as carried out, what is carried out a little is made out as much, what is carried out much is made out as little, one thing is carried out while another is made out (as carried out), what is carried out from one source is made out as from another, what is to be paid is not paid, what is not to be paid is paid, payment is not made in time, payment is made untimely, a little paid is made out as much, what is overpaid is made out as little, one thing is given while another is made out as given, what is paid to one is made out as paid to another, what is delivered (into the treasury) is made out as not delivered, what is not delivered is made out as delivered, forest produce for which the price has not been paid is delivered, forest produce for which the price has not been paid is delivered, that for which the price has been paid is not delivered, concentration (of goods) is made out as dispersal, or dispersal made out as concentration, an object of high value is changed for one of low value, or one of low value for one of high value, the price is raised, or (the

> price is) reduced, the year is made discrepant as to months, or the month discrepant as to days, discrepancy as to source, discrepancy as to head (of income etc.), discrepancy as to workmen, discrepancy in performance, discrepancy in the sum-total, discrepancy in quality, discrepancy in price, discrepancy in weighing, discrepancy in measuring, (and) discrepancy as to (container) vessels—these are the (forty) ways of embezzlement.

He further advises on how to handle these cases:

> In these cases, he should interrogate, each individually, the subordinate officer, the store-keeper, the recorder, the receiver, the person who pays, the person who causes the payment to be made, the adviser and the help-mate. And in case of a false statement by these, the fine shall be the same as for the officer (concerned). And he should issue a proclamation in the sphere of his activity. Those wronged by such and such an officer should communicate (it to me), to such as communicate, he should cause payment to be made in accordance with the injury suffered.

Arthashastra was a result of wisdom of centuries of work done by different scholars. It offered advice to the king on various issues of law, selection of Ministers and extensive use of agents who collected information from people. Chanakya felt that "just as it is impossible not to taste honey," it was not possible for government servants not to eat up at least a bit of king's revenue. And he realised that it was very difficult to find out whether this erosion in revenue had happened. He gave the simile of a fish while floating in water and observed that whether it was drinking or not drinking water was difficult to find. He felt very strongly on protecting the treasury from corrupt officials. He, therefore, warned that "it is possible to know the path of birds flying in the sky, but not the ways of officers moving with their intentions concealed." In several areas of governance and the prescriptive policies, morality and ethics was not considered supreme. The end was more important than the means to achieve it.[2]

Even in subsequent years, in kingdoms across the country, this issue was considered important by the Sultans and Mughal rulers. When the East India Company came and set up shops in India, there were complaints of extensive corruption in its functioning. Lord Clive who was considered as the architect of establishing British Rule and making a strong base for East India Company was accused of corruption.[3]

Corruption in the Initial Years of Independence

The Independence struggle saw leaders of great probity and integrity emerge in public life. However, corruption in the governance structure was rather strong. Jawaharlal Nehru, even before taking office as head of the interim government in September 1946, attacked "the colossal corruption and nepotism rampant everywhere." He observed that "corrupt people have to be swept away by a broomstick."[4] In the Constituent Assembly, while framing the Indian Constitution, the debates do not, however, reflect the issues relating to corruption and setting up of an institutional mechanism as strongly. However, they were acutely conscious of the need for integrity in public life. While emphasising the need for this, Dr Rajendra Prasad on 26 November 1949 had said:[5]

> If the people who are elected are capable and men of character and integrity they would be able to make the best even of a defective Constitution. If they are lacking in these the Constitution cannot help the country. It is up to us to preserve and protect the independence that we have won and to make it bear fruit for the man in the street. Let us launch on this new enterprise of running our Independent Republic with confidence, with truth and non-violence and above all with heart within and God over head.

While discussing qualifications of Members of Parliament (MPs) and of ministers, the issue came up whether such corrupt person could become eligible to be elected to the Parliament. There was unanimous feeling that we must not permit any laxity on this score. The issue of corruption was at that point extremely critical. Gunnar Myrdal (1968: 702-05) in his book *Asian Drama: An Inquiry into the Poverty of Nations* dealt with this issue extensively. He mentions:[6]

> In India and Ceylon, Ceylon especially, but also in other South Asian countries, the authorities have, from the start of the independence era, tried to prevent corruption, and

> these efforts have, on the whole, been increasing. Yet the articulate in all these countries believe that corruption is rampant and that it is growing, particularly among higher officials and politicians, including legislators and ministers. The ostentations efforts to prevent corruption and the assertions that the corrupt are being dealt with as they deserve only seem to spread cynicism, especially as to how far all this touches the "higher-ups."

The issues of corruption continued to be an important issue of governance during this period. Two such cases need specific mention. First one is related to the import of jeeps (1948). There were allegations that V.K. Krishna Menon, the then Indian High Commissioner to Britain, bypassed standard procedures and signed a deal for purchase of army jeeps for ₹80 lakhs with a foreign firm. It seems that army urgently required 4,000 jeeps in Kashmir after the outbreak of hostilities due to foreign aggression. After due negotiations, orders for 2,000 old re-conditioned jeeps were placed on a firm in London. It was planned in these orders that supply will be completed in three years and five months. Spares were also to be given. Shipment was started in December 1948. Only 155 re-conditioned jeeps were supplied by March 1949. These, however, were found to be unserviceable by the army. Further, 65 per cent of the amount was paid to the supplier, though it was to be given after receipt of inspection certificate of the jeeps proposed for supply. There were several other gaps. The amount was paid within one month instead of 65 days. The inspection agency was changed and spares were reduced to 10 per cent of the originally planned. The contract had been negotiated by Menon, and Defence Ministry officials were not willing to support it. Criticism of the deal made by PAC which had suggested an enquiry by a High Court Judge was ignored. It seems that one E.H. Potter was an agent in all the deals negotiated by Menon. Menon had a record of impeccable integrity. The case was, therefore, closed in 1955. It is, however, instructive to cover this case for an important reason. Since the reputation of Menon for honesty was well accepted, no one questioned Nehru's motive on the issue in spite of the fact that there were gross violations of procedures.

The other case of corruption of this period involving financial mismanagement has been referred to as Mundra scandal. Haridas

Mundra was a Calcutta based businessperson. He sold fraudulent shares to Life Insurance Corporation (LIC). Feroze Gandhi, the husband of former Prime Minister (PM) Indira Gandhi, raised the question in the Parliament about the share deal. PM Nehru constituted a one-member commission headed by Justice M.C. Chagla to enquire into the matter. The Commission concluded that there was a *prima facie* case against Mundra of selling fictitious shares to LIC and defrauding it to the extent of ₹1.25 crore. Mundra was convicted and sentenced to a long imprisonment and T.T. Krishnamachari (TTK), the then Finance Minister, was obliged to quit the Cabinet owning moral responsibility.[7]

It became increasingly evident that the issue of corruption had to be addressed in a more systematic manner and a new institution was required to address corruption, amongst senior officials and ministers. A Committee on prevention of corruption under Santhanam, a distinguished public figure, was appointed in the above context in the 1960s. The Santhanam Committee did extensive work, examined the extent of corruption and concluded that the corruption was not confined to the lower ranks of public service and the number of cases in which gazetted officers were involved was alarming. In its assessments, corruption was a complex problem having roots and ramifications in society as a whole. It, therefore, made several recommendations. These included setting up of the Central Vigilance Commission (CVC) for enquiring into complaints against government officials. Following these recommendations, the CVC was set up in 1964. The Committee also suggested a code of conduct for central and state ministers, MPs, Members of Legislative Assemblies (MLAs), and also for political parties. The code of conduct for ministers was to include same provisions as applicable to public servants in respect of acquisition of property, acceptance of gifts and discloser of assets and liabilities. It also made suggestions on fund raising which would lead to prevention of corrupt practices.

The Santhanam Committee also recommended that the President might constitute, on the advice of the PM, a national panel out of which a committee of three persons may be constituted to enquire into the allegations against a minister. At least, one of the three persons should have held or should be holding a high judicial office.

The committee constituted out of the national panel should first ascertain whether there is a *prima facie* case. It should have the power to direct the Central Bureau of Investigation (CBI) to investigate and report. If the Committee wishes to make some enquiries other than through the CBI, it should be given the necessary facilities. If a formal allegation is made by any 10 MPs in writing to the PM through the Speaker (Lok Sabha) or the Chairman (Rajya Sabha), the PM should consider himself obliged, by convention, to refer the allegation for immediate investigation by such a committee. Unfortunately, many of the recommendations on enquiries against ministers were not implemented.

Corruption in delivery of public services, in award of large contracts and in large purchases continued unabated in spite of the above observations of the Committee. Large funds transferred by the Planning Commission for various development schemes could not be utilised effectively due to leakages and corruption at various levels. The extent of this was so glaring that the former PM Rajiv Gandhi in mid-1980s famously remarked that out of every rupee spent on development schemes only 15 paisa reached the poor. The observations only highlighted the fact that the delivery system was very poor, inefficient and corrupt. The statement shocked the nation but very little effective new instruments were worked out or systemic changes made to address this problem.

The corruption in the initial four decades post-independence had its root in several areas. First, the economy was of shortages and distribution, therefore, invariably resulted in pilferage. The public distribution system (PDS) leaked badly. In other areas too where efforts were made to distribute commodities which were in short supply like the yarn (1973), edible oil and vanaspati (1973-1975) and fertilisers, there were complaints of corruption. Second, large purchases were involved in defence contracts. Invariably, in these, some middlemen tried to make money while acting as agents. Efforts of the central government to ban use of agents in defence contracts did not succeed. It was interesting that the Government of India (GoI) employed agents abroad for selling its own exports. This was clearly not a practical arrangement to ban agents completely in India while other countries sold their equipment. These agents, therefore, continued in some form or the other—agent, advisor, informal representative or an employee. Third, the economy had large tariff barriers. It was, therefore, quite profitable to smuggle goods as it saved enormous amount of custom duty. It promoted inefficient production as there was no incentive for the manufacturers to reduce costs. This also led to misuse of export and import regulations which were quite complex. The transaction cost in these complex web of regulations and large tariff barriers was quite high. Some liberalisation took place in the 1980s but it was quite inadequate. Fourth, very little systemic reformers were introduced during this period. As cost of fighting elections went up, political corruption expanded further. The electoral process, however, did not result in any laws which could reduce corruption. Fifth, the procedures for delivery of public services continued to be complex. This, therefore, did not result in any reduction in corruption as transaction cost for delivering the service was realised by government officials. Corruption continued to thrive in award of large purchases including defence and delivery of public services by the government. Two important cases of corruption came in for public debate relating to defence purchases during this period. The purchase of Bofors guns, a deal worth ₹ 1,650 crore was criticised on the ground that there was indeed a middleman and bribes had been paid. Cases went on in the Indian courts and the Swiss courts. The CBI who had investigated the matter filed charge sheets. There were allegations that money had been paid to the former PM Rajiv Gandhi. The case, however, did not result in conviction of any individual. Allegations against the former PM, Rajiv Gandhi, were not proved. There was another case relating to import of HDW submarines from Germany. In this case too, there were allegations of corruption. Both these cases attracted a lot of media attention, public debate and enormous political polemics and in this case, too, none was convicted.

The Bofors Gun purchases and HDW submarine cases were symptoms of the weak Indian governance system and inadequate political will to address issues of corruption. Prior to that, there were allegations of corruption in Commerce Ministry. Similar allegations were made in respect of corruption in export of rice to the USSR with which we had a special trade balancing arrangement. In many of these instances, it was stated that commissions were collected. However, the fundamental question was never discussed as to how to tighten the system and stop leakages and corruption. S.S. Gill (1998), who was Secretary to GoI, expresses serious concern on political corruption:

> But I am convinced that this affliction cannot be effectively tackled by prescribing rules of conduct and other mechanical means. Corruption can come only from the political class, which has the financial, legislative and executive authority in a parliamentary democracy. The waywardness of our politicians can be curbed only from within. There is no agency which can improve polity from outside. Unless the politicians educate themselves to clearly differentiate private conscience from public morality and personal profit from national interest, the ongoing plunder of the national exchequer cannot be stopped.[8]

The Era of Reforms

The 1990s saw major economic reforms. The economy was facing difficult situation as the balance of payment (BoP) position was difficult and foreign exchange reserves had reduced to one month of requirement. The reforms led to major changes in the tariff structure. The measures taken in this era were quite extensive. First, the tariff rates were reduced to moderate levels and these were planned to be reduced further subsequently. Second, the rupee was devalued and the new foreign currency rates were closer to the market. Third, the export and import regulations were drastically curtailed. Fourth, private investments and foreign direct investments were promoted in a large number of areas. This opened up the economy to greater international competition and helped it to become more competitive.

The economic reforms led to dismantling of the licence permit *raj*, imports and exports had far less restrictions, and tariff rates were reduced drastically. This helped elimination of huge transaction costs and corruption in which many players were engaged in. Greater integration with the market and globalisation led to improved competition with the international players. This was a very positive step in reducing corruption inherent in the system. The policies also had a very positive impact on the growth process. The rates of GDP growth in 1950-1980 were averaging 3.5 per cent. In the 1980s, it increased to 5.0-5.5 per cent. In the 1990s, growth started picking up. In 1990-2000, average growth was 6.5 per cent. Subsequently in 2000-2010, it accelerated further to 7.5 per cent.[9] The higher growth rates, thus, were a direct result of the economic reforms undertaken in the 1990s. These also eliminated the corruption inherent in the licence permit regime, as mentioned earlier.

While the economic growth resulted in an effective check on one source of corruption, the growth process unleashed other forces which led to subsequent problems. The policies on economic growth envisaged large investments by private sectors and opening up of the economy for this. It involved development of infrastructure and focus on manufacturing. In many cases, it also envisaged allocation of natural resources to private companies: spectrum for communication, coal mines for steel, cement and power plants, iron ore mines for development of steel mills for iron and steel, land for development of airports and sea ports and similar other allocations. In the initial decade, as the private sector investments started coming in these areas, there was not enough competition. The policies of allocation of these resources, therefore, did not attract much criticism. Most of these were made by the central government depending upon needs of the industry.

During 2000-2010, economy picked up and the size of the GDP increased to more than trillion dollars. Growth rates in certain years crossed nine per cent. The demand and ensuing competition for natural resources increased. This led to corruption in several ways. First, the system of allocation itself, even when through high powered committees, was sought to be subverted by many private players by giving wrong information or trying to influence the committee's deliberation. Second, the method of allocation like the allotment in the 2G spectrum was attempted to be subverted by some players through questionable means. There were allegations in this regard about the decision taken at the ministerial level. On these issues, cases have been filed in the court. The issue was also considered at the highest judicial level in the Supreme Court and in the Parliament and a Joint Parliament Committee (JPC) was subsequently appointed which gave its report.[10]

Third, it was alleged that the method of allocations were not in the interest of the state exchequer as it led to losses. The argument was that the national resources should have been priced at market prices, but were given away at low rates. This, it was argued, had led to corruption. Fourth, it was stated that whatever the government policy, the allocations since not done on an auction basis had resulted in corrupt practices. In the case of allocation of spectrum, the Comptroller and Auditor General (CAG) in its report computed a presumptive loss of ₹ 1.76 lakh crore. In the case of coal allocation also in another CAG report, it was stated that undue profit accrued to private mine allottee in steel, cement and power sectors and involved a loss of ₹ 1.86 lakh crore. Both these, thus, were high profile cases of alleged corruption.[11]

While reforming of the economy led to dismantling of the licence permit *raj*, there were other opportunities resulting from larger private investment and participation in the economy. With the increase in size of the budget, government expenditure also increased in a number of schemes, especially in the social sector. While one set of policies helped reduce corruption, new private sector investments and large government expenditure resulting from higher growth opened new opportunities for corruption. The corruption level in the country during 1996-2012, the period for which the indices for measuring corruption were available, indicated no reduction in corruption in terms of the World Bank index. The Corruption Perceptions Index (CPI) prepared by the Transparency International (TI), however, showed a lower corruption.[12]

The implication of the above data is clear. Corruption in this period as a share of GDP either remained static or had gone down very marginally as indicated by the index. However, since the GDP had in the meanwhile increased quite substantially from $483 billion in 1996 to $1.46 trillion in 2012, in US dollar as well in Indian rupee terms, the corruption showed a dramatic increase.[13] Corruption in India is widespread in terms of its reach and includes both petty and political corruption. In many developing economies, political and petty corruptions often overlap. Petty corruption benefits are often shared amongst politicians, contractors and government officials. This sharing may be direct or indirect. In the first category, the contractor or government official shares the part of bribe with the political class. In the second category, there is no immediate sharing with politician. But the government official agrees to appoint contractors or award contracts in a corrupt manner to persons indicated by the political master. The bribe is then settled with the contractor by the politician.

Table 6.1

Corruption in India

Years	*CPI (Transparency International)*	*Corruption Index (World Bank)*
1996	2.63	-0.402
1998	2.90	-0.283
2000	2.8	-0.365
2001	2.7	NA
2002	2.7	-0.497
2003	2.8	-0.436
2004	2.8	-0.413
2005	2.9	-0.397
2006	3.3	-0.297
2007	3.5	-0.425
2008	3.4	-0.361
2009	3.4	-0.478
2010	3.3	-0.512
2011	3.1	-0.572
2012	3.6	-0.565

Note: Transparency International Index (TII) is on the 0-10 scale. Lower index means higher corruption. The World Bank is on -2.5 to +2.5 scale. Lower values indicate higher corruption. World Bank did not report corruption data for the year 2001.

Robert Wade in his perspectives *Corruption: Where Does the Money Go?* mentions about corruption in police, irrigation and revenue Departments. He refers to a South Indian state where post of State Superintendent is put for auction and the winner pays to the minister. He has a year to collect his investment and make profit. He collects it from his subordinates, who also get their choice of posting. Similar corruption strategy is adopted by irrigation engineers, revenue department and Public Works Department (PWD), etc. Poor governance and personnel policy is at the root of corruption.[14] Details of well-structured mechanism of corruption have been given by Debroy and

Bhandari (2012). They mention a commission of 13-15 per cent, of which 5-10 per cent goes to the minister in irrigation projects in special division. The detailed methodology of vertically integrated corruption structure, where corruption proceeds are shared by functionaries at different levels in the chain, given by them indicates how corruption has become an integral part of administration in these areas.[15]

Several studies have been made on extent of corruption in India in different departments of the government, especially of states. TI in collaboration with Centre for Media Studies (CMS) have in 2005 and later made an assessment of corruption in different states of India. These results indicate that the three most corrupt departments in the states are police, judiciary (lower) and land administration. The other departments in order of corruption were municipal works, hospitals, electricity and PDS. They also assessed that amongst the states, Bihar has the highest level of corruption (2005) and Kerala the least (Table 6.2).

The Transparency International study estimated that the total value of petty corruption in the 11 services, which it had studied, was ₹21,068 crore ($4.2 billion) annually. The estimates of bribes paid were highest in school education. It indicated bribes of ₹4,137 crore in school education, ₹3,899 crore in police, ₹3,126 crore in land administration and lower judiciary of ₹2,630 crore. Interestingly, school education which ranked lower in perception of corruption showed a high monetary value. This was ascribed to a very large number of people interacting with the school education system.[16]

According to Debroy and Bhandari (2012), it is estimated that public servants in India may be getting richer annually by an estimated $18.42 billion or 1.26 per cent of the India's GDP.[17] The highest bribery were paid, as estimated by them, in transport industry, real estate and some services provided by the government. The extent of corruption prevalent in different departments of the government is strongly influenced by nature of clients or citizens and their urgency for a favourable decision. Both police and judiciary fall in this category. An adverse decision may land the person in jail or he may lose his land and other assets. They have made an assessment of anti-corruption efforts in different states and found Bihar, Gujarat, Andhra Pradesh and Punjab as the best and Odisha, Assam, Jharkhand and West Bengal as the worst States in terms of their indices. Some other studies have made slightly different conclusions. Ernst & Young (2013) has estimated that infrastructure, real estate, aerospace and defence, and power utilities had the highest level of corruption.[18] Another study done by KPMG (2011) indicates real estates, telecommunication, and social development projects as prone to highest level of corruption.[19] Clearly, two sectors get identified—first, real estate; second, infrastructure including transport.

Table 6.2

Corruption in Indian States

States	*Corruption Index Score*
Kerala	240
Himachal Pradesh	301
Gujarat	417
Andhra Pradesh	421
Maharashtra	433
Chhattisgarh	445
Punjab	459
West Bengal	461
Odisha	475
Uttar Pradesh	491
Delhi	496
Tamil Nadu	509
Haryana	516
Jharkhand	520
Assam	542
Rajasthan	548
Karnataka	576
Madhya Pradesh	584
Jammu & Kashmir	685
Bihar	695

Note: Lower index means lower corruption.

A large number of cases in the last three decades have engaged public attention. There have been allegations of corruption in all these. During discussions the cases were generally referred to as scandals. Some of these were: Cement Scandal in Maharashtra involving allegations against former CM of Maharashtra (1982), HDW submarine scam (1980s), Bofors gun scandal (1986), animal husbandry scam involving former CMs of Bihar (1996), telecom scandal involving former Telecom Minister (1996), Telgi stamp scam (1995), Satyam scam (2008), CWG scam (2010), cash for votes scandal involving former PM (1996), 2G scam and coal block allocation scam involving ministers and bureaucrats (2006-2011). The cases mentioned above involving politicians and senior civil servants are in public domain and have been referred to in recent works on corruption in detail. The erosion of people's faith in our governance system and the environment of venality and extortion that it promoted did far greater harm than the losses to the exchequer or the enrichment of individuals which may have happened.[20]

Recent debates on corruption have focused on, apart from above factors, the black money, especially in Swiss Banks. The initial reports were of large illegal deposits in Swiss Banks. A report published in May 2012 sourcing information from Swiss National Bank, however, indicates that the total deposits by Indian nationals in 2010 were $2.1 billion. A similar estimate was given by Dev Kar who indicated that estimates of $1.4 trillion were way off the mark.[21] The government has recently appointed a Special Investigating Team (SIT) under former Supreme Court Judge M.B. Shah to bring back money which is deposited illegally with foreign banks. It is clearly a difficult task. But political will is going to be a key factor in this.

Anti-Corruption Strategy

There is no document or policy paper which could be termed as a comprehensive anti-corruption strategy in India. There are, however, a set of laws, vigilance institutions and investigative machinery. Based on the result of investigation, police or special agencies file charge sheets in courts. There are a number of government orders advising ministries on actions which would reduce corruption. We shall look at some of the important intervention made to reduce corruption.

The anti-corruption efforts in India are spearheaded by CVC along with CBI as an investigating agency. The CVC was set up in 1964 consequent upon implementation of the recommendations of the Santhanam Committee. The CVC Act was passed in 2003 and the office of CVC was further strengthened. In the states, the policies to control corruption are supported by anti-corruption wing in police departments and Lokayukta to varying extent. The major legislation defining corruption, bribery and mandating punishment is Prevention of Corruption Act, 1988, which defines corruption, public servants and the punishment for various offences given in the act. In addition to provisions in the Indian Panel Court (1860), certain provisions relating to tax evasions in the Income Tax Act 1961 and the Prevention of Money Laundering Act 2002 also specify various offences punishable for corrupt behaviour. The Benami Transaction (Prohibition) Act 1988 has prohibited transactions which are *benami* and provided punishment in these cases.

The CVC Act 2003 provides for a central vigilance commissioner with two vigilance commissioners. The central vigilance commissioner is to be selected by a committee presided over by the PM and includes Leader of Opposition and Home Minister. There are also vigilance officers in every organisation. Generally, an officer working in the Department is designated as vigilance officer. In bigger offices and PSUs (public sector undertakings), there are whole-time vigilance officers. On receipt of complaints, the central vigilance commissioner enquires into it and recommends disciplinary action or may order investigation by CBI, the central investigation agency.

The CBI was set up under Delhi Police Establishment Act, 1946. Initially, it was constituted under an executive order in 1941 and later brought under the act. Possibly, the large-scale corruption during the war period brought urgency to this issue. The question of independence of CBI while investigating these cases has been a central point of debate. Since it can investigate corruption cases against all central public servants, unless these are conducted fairly and expeditiously, the effectiveness of anti-corruption efforts gets weakened. Serious questions have been raised on this issue. Political interference and slow pace of investigation have led to serious delays in convictions.

Sukh Ram, former Telecom Minister and Lalu Prasad Yadav, former Chief Minister of Bihar were convicted more than 15 years after the charges had come in public domain.

The system for eradication of corruption in the states is quite separate. They generally have an anti-corruption wing in the Department of Police. A number of states have passed a Lokayukta Act. Most states, which have the act, have included CM and ministers in its ambit. The appointment of the Lokayukta, who is generally a retired Supreme Court or High Court judge, is made with approval of the governor. In a number of states like Karnataka and Madhya Pradesh, the Lokayukta has its own police to launch raids to investigate, search and seize documents. States which, have not set up Lokayukta include Arunachal Pradesh, Manipur, Meghalaya, Mizoram, Nagaland, Sikkim, Tripura, Jammu & Kashmir (J&K), West Bengal and Tamil Nadu. Northeastern states, Tamil Nadu and West Bengal are notable exceptions, apart from J&K. Considering that several northeastern states have set up joint power regulators, it may be appropriate for them to set up one Lokayukta covering two or three states. But not setting up of Lokayukta institutions in these states is not appropriate, as large government funds are being transferred to the region and there are serious complaints of misuse and corruption. It is also important for J&K and Tamil Nadu, which figure in the bottom half of TI study of 2005 on levels of corruption in states. It also indicates lack of concern for accountability of public officials and disregard for reducing corruption.

An important instrument for preventing corruption is a watch by public spirited individuals of corrupt practices of organisations or individuals. The system has been well accepted in the US. Just before the change of government in May 2014, The Whistle Blowers Protection Bill, 2011 became a law in India. This act provides protection to any person who makes a public interest disclosure before a public authority. The act also provides for a person to make a public interest disclosure before a competent authority or central vigilance commissioner. Malafide disclosures, however, are to be discouraged with a provision of fine and imprisonment up to two years. The act should provide another instrument to prevent corruption.

An effective mechanism for controlling and preventing corruption is promoting transparency. Several legislations and policy interventions have been made in the recent years in states and central government. All these have an impact on preventing corruption. The most significant of these is the Right to Information (RTI) Act, 2005. This give right to every citizen to get information from any public office, including judicial offices, with some exceptions primarily on grounds of national security. The act prescribes time-limits for providing information and makes officers individually liable for fines. All states have also similarly set up offices to implement this law. The RTI Act promotes transparency and accountability. In most respects, it is one of the most progressive legislations, though because of its very wide sweep, it has been misused extensively more for private gains and less for promoting public purposes.

The second set of legislations promoting good governance, which reduces avenues for corrupt acts, are on delivery of public services in a prescribed time frame. A number of states, including Madhya Pradesh, Delhi and Chhattisgarh have passed the legislation. The central government had introduced a bill in Parliament referred to as 'The Right of Citizens for Time Bound Delivery of Goods and Services and Redressal of their Grievances Bill, 2011'. Due to dissolution of the Lower House of Parliament or Lok Sabha, it lapsed. The Bill had sought to confer a right on all citizens to get time-bound delivery of public services. It also made it mandatory for every public authority to publish a citizens' charter, which would give details of services in the concerned department. This was planned to be completed in six months. The Bill provided for fines from officials' salary and for disciplinary proceedings in case of failure.

The Bill also included provisions similar to RTI Act 2005 on grievance redressal officer, appellate authority and state/central public grievance redressal commissions. In addition, where designated authority was of the view that corruption may be involved in the complaint, he could refer it to the competent authority for taking action under the Prevention of Corruption Act, 1988. It will improve governance if the bill is taken up again for early passage.

The Lokpal Act

Efforts have been made in the last four decades to set up the institution of Lokpal. In absence of political will, these have failed. Recent discussions and public debates on setting up the office of Lokpal to investigate and prosecute corrupt public servants has resulted in the passage of the act. The enactment called the Lokpal and Lokayukta Act, 2013 was passed by the parliament in December 2013 and received the presidential assent on 1 January, 2014. The Act aims to set up a mechanism for enquiries and investigation of officers engaged in corruption. It enables corruption charges to be filed in court against PM, ministers, MPs, secretaries to GoI and other officials. The Lokpal will not require any permission to prosecute civil servants accused of corrupt acts. The Act provides for selection of the Lokpal by an independent process. It empowers the Lokpal to conduct enquiries and ask CBI to investigate charges of corruption, and also has a power to prosecute them. The Act provides for eight members of the Lokpal and a chairperson to be selected through a very transparent process. Half of the members are expected to be judicial members. The act also provides that at least half of the total members will be from OBC (other backward class), ST (scheduled tribe)/SC (scheduled caste) and women. It also provides for opportunities to charged officials to present his case before a view is taken during enquiries. In addition to provisions for the Lokpal, the act also mentions setting up of Lokayukta in every state for dealing with complaints of corruption against public servants of the state. A time period of one year from the commencement of the Act is prescribed during which this enactment is to be passed by the states. It does not, however, suggest any special provision which should be included in the Lokayukta Act.

CBI, as mentioned earlier, will continue to be the premier investigating agency of the government for all important cases of corruption and crime. The Director, CBI, is to be appointed, under the above Act, by a committee chaired by the PM and including leader of the opposition in Lok Sabha and Chief Justice of India or his representative. The rest of the officers of the CBI, above the rank of Superintendent of Police, are to be selected by a committee presided over by the central vigilance commissioner (CVC). The selection process thus ensures that a fair and independent selection is made. The investigations of CBI are to be supervised by CVC and the Lokpal as may be prescribed by general or special order by the Lokpal. The Lokpal Act authorises Lokpal to set up its own wing for conducting enquiries and for this purpose Director of Enquiries and Director of Prosecution are to be appointed by the Lokpal. The Lokpal has to set up his own procedures in respect of decisions to be made by it. However every Lokpal bench, which will consider issues placed before it, will have at least one judicial member.

The Lokpal Act provides that in respect of Class C and D categories of officials, the decisions may be taken by the Central Vigilance Commissioner after receipt of the Enquiry Report or a report sent by CBI whether to launch prosecution or to take departmental action. The investigation will also be supervised by the CVC.

The Act has several positive features. It ensures independence in selection of Lokpal. The selection committee is to be chaired by the PM with Chief Justice of India or his nominee as one of the members, leader of opposition in the Lok Sabha, speaker of Lok Sabha and an eminent jurist as one of the members. The jurist is to be appointed by the President based on recommendations of the other four members. The Act also is fairly wide in covering the persons against whom investigations and enquiries can be done. Thus, the PM, all ministers as well as the senior civil servants can be investigated through independent investigations. It is also provided that in case of corrupt public servants, confiscation of property apart from imprisonment up to seven years can be made. To ensure checks and balances approach, the investigations of CBI are to be supervised by the CVC and Lokpal. To guard against false and frivolous allegations, there is a provision for prosecution of those who indulge in this.

There has been criticism of the Lokpal Bill on several counts. One of the important areas of criticism is the fact that it does not cover cases like Jharkhand Mukti Morcha (JMM) bribery case, where votes were purchased for running the government. It has been argued that since the way MPs vote is not the domain of judiciary but of Parliament itself, no prosecution can be made of such MPs. Considering that we want to make a good clean government with high level of democratic values, it is important that mechanism is created for enquiry into these cases. Experience of other countries, including Italy, the US and the UK has shown that for healthy functioning of democracy, this is essential. In the 18th century in the UK, MPs' votes could be purchased. In Italy, a few years back, PM Berlusconi was charged with buying a house member by offering bribe to him to defeat, a charge which was later proved. In the US, it is not unknown for the President to offer incentives to buy support of Senators or members of House of Representatives. In India, former PM P.V. Narsimha Rao was charged with buying of votes. Recently these allegations were made against the United Progressive Alliance (UPA) Government. Lokpal could be authorised by the Parliament to enquire into these cases after passing an appropriate law or if necessary making a suitable provision in the Constitution. Based on the Lokpal's report, Parliament can launch criminal prosecution and dismiss the member.

The Act has also been criticised on the ground that while the CBI directors are to be appointed by a committee headed by the PM and not changed for a period, other senior officials of CBI are to be appointed by the government on a CVC committee recommendation. There is no provision that concurrence of Lokpal is required for their transfer except where they are investigating a case given by Lokpal. For curtailing tenure of other senior officers, permission of CVC committee is required. Considering that the CBI is the main investigating agency and the investigating officers will be the main instrument, it is essential that they remain independent and do not work under the control of government. It would have been useful, if there were provisions that concurrence of Lokpal or CVC may be needed for shifting officers from CBI. It is important that investigating officers do not feel threatened by transfer when conducting investigations against senior civil servants and powerful politicians even when their tenure is over and the case has not come to CBI through Lokpal. Powers of transfer with government hence needs to be exercised only on proposals sent by Lokpal.

The Act has also been criticised on the ground that it provides for timelines for prosecution of cases and investigation. It is not clear as to what will happen if these timelines are exceeded. This is a purely clarificatory issue and needs to be appropriately handled by the government.

An important provision in the Act is investigation of complaints against the PM. There are provisions for appropriate exclusions of areas of enquiry on grounds of external and internal security, public order, atomic energy and space. There is also a requirement that unless two-third of members of Lokpal agree, such an enquiry need not be taken up. We consider it appropriate that in the initial years these safeguards are kept. It will be, however, necessary to review these provisions once certain traditions relating to functioning of Lokpal are established. We could consider a sunset clause of a decade after which modified and less stringent provisions could be introduced for undertaking such an enquiry.

There has also been a criticism of the Act regarding no template about setting up anti-corruption machinery in the states. The Act only mentions that Lokayukta will be set up in the states within one year of commencement of the Act. Already there are 19 states which have Lokayukta Act. The provisions in these acts vary widely. It would have been far more effective to suggest a model Lokayukta Act and then leave it to the states for considering it on merits. Unfortunately, even the states have considered this as encroaching on their territory. As a consequence, very bland provisions have been put. This is not conducive to lowering corruption in states.

Constitutional Safeguards

Independence of institutions, especially of audit, is a key policy intervention to keep a check on financial misappropriation and financial discipline. CAG, the chief auditor of the government, is an independent institutional office under the Constitution and is responsible for auditing of accounts of all central and state government undertakings, offices and organisations under these governments. The independence of the auditor ensures that they are able to work without any interference from the government and thus provide a complete picture of the accounts of concerned governments. In the recent years, this issue gained importance when a number of controversial reports were given by the CAG relating to defence purchases and allotment of natural resources. In the case of Bofors, the then CAG gave his observations which resulted in criminal investigations into the gun purchase. Similarly, in the 2G spectrum and coal blocks, the CAG gave his report based on which subsequent CBI investigations were undertaken. A JPC was also formed on 2G issue. As is well known, these became major issues where serious allegations of corruption were widely discussed. In spite of the fact that CAG is appointed by the President based on recommendations of the PM, and no transparent process is in existence for recommending a panel, the system has worked well. These officers have been fairly independent in their reports to the parliament. It will be however necessary to have a more transparent procedure in appointment of CAG to further strengthen this independence.

An important institution whose working has very major impact on corruption, especially political corruption, is the office of Election Commission. This constitutional office, including the Chief Election Commissioner (CEC) and the Election Commissioners (ECs), is responsible for conducting free and fair elections in the country both for states as well as the central legislatures. In this, they have succeeded quite well. However, over a period of years, an important concern has been the use of money power in the elections. While the commission has fixed the limit of expenses by candidates, political parties spend a lot of money in the elections. Since this is primarily provided by business houses, they exercise enormous influence over the framing of policies. Such policies under the influence of business houses have a strong potential of favouring those who have provided the money during the elections. It is necessary that this influence of money power is curbed. It has, however, important implications for corruption since many of the public representatives spend a lot of money on fighting election. When they win a seat in the Parliament, there is a very strong temptation to recoup all the money spent in fighting the election. This leads to a lot of political corruption and distorts public policy. The Election Commission has functioned independently over the last several decades. It has suggested reforms in the electoral process on several occasions. By strengthening the provisions of model code of conduct, it has been partially successful in controlling the influence of money power in elections. Several reforms are needed in the process. The role of money in elections, adequate representation to women and keeping criminal elements out of the parliament are much needed reforms. It is important that integrity of our electoral process is made stronger by selection of CEC and ECs through a transparent mechanism.

Technology

The efforts to curb corruption have been supplemented by some other initiatives aimed at simplifying procedures for delivery of public services and thereby reducing scope for transaction cost or bribery. Most of these relate to use of IT and adoption of best practices. Central government has in its key initiative started an e-governance plan in 27 areas. They have also started connecting the *panchayats* with optical fiber cables to improve connectivity. An important initiative has been to set up common service centres where a number of citizen services are available through private sectors.

Several state governments, especially Andhra Pradesh and Chhattisgarh, are using IT in delivery of public services. Some of the major initiatives in this area include railway reservation system, net–banking, e-Governance plan for 27 areas including MCA-21 and passport services and other services using Aadhar Card. e-Governance plan has succeeded in states with better record of governance and corruption. Jennifer Russell points out in her study that "politicians in those states with higher level of petty corruption were more likely to delay implementation of these policies, or not implement them at all, than leaders of less corrupt States."[22] She feels that states led by coalition governments implemented these policies with delay (or not at all) as compared to single-party states. This highlights the importance of stable governments. Her study also confirms that states with higher level of corruption tend to provide fewer services at CSC (common services centres), leaving those with higher corruption potential outside the reach of CSC.

Use of technology for improving public service delivery is extremely important and a key intervention for reducing corruption. It has enabled a fresh look at existing procedures by using IT-enabled delivery and simplified systems. The petty corruption is rampant at the grass-roots level. It is these services whose availability has to be simplified and made corruption-free.

Independent Monitors

It is possible to reduce corruption by effective third-party monitoring and social audit of public programmes. This strategy has been used successfully in Pradhan Mantri Gram Sadak Yojana (PMGSY).[23] By March 2012, nearly 300,000 kms of roads had been made and there were very few complaints of corruption. All these were rural roads, made *pucca* and involved extensive construction throughout the country. Due to a system of three tier monitoring by independent monitors, the complaints were minimised and the quality of work was excellent. The programme evaluation organisation of the Planning Commission found extensive appreciation for this work.

The third party monitoring was also introduced in some projects in northeastern region (NER). There had been reports of large-scale leakage of funds in the rural areas in the northeastern states. It was not possible to inspect different works in the region due to difficult terrain, long distances involved, nature of works which were in remote areas and of very small in value, making monitoring difficult and uneconomic. A system of third party monitoring was introduced during the Eleventh Plan (2007-2012) in several states. The works were inspected by NABARD Consultancy Organisation (NABCONS) and North East Development Finance Corporation (NEDFI) selected for this purpose. The reports showed large number of deficiencies in the work done. These were then brought to the notice of the concerned districts. These deficiencies or incomplete work or poor quality work were then set right and were again inspected and so certified. Although there was a strong opposition, it has helped improve the quality of works. The employment of third party monitors, thus acts as a check on misuse of funds. The concept of social audit has been introduced in recent times for works done under Mahatma Gandhi National Rural Employment Guarantee Act (MGNREGA). It is is also useful for all village level works. It involves support of independent civil society organisations. It is a good watch over works in rural areas.

Second Administrative Reforms Commission (ARC) Recommendations

The issue of curtailing corruption has been extensively discussed by ARC in its fourth report on "Ethics in Governance". It has suggested a series of recommendations. These include:[24]

(a) Partial state funding of elections.
(b) Disqualification of anti-defectors to be decided by the President/Governor on the advice of Election Commission.
(c) Setting up of an office of Ethics Commissioner to advise the Speaker/Chairman.
(d) Prescribing code of ethics for Ministers and its monitoring by PM/Chief Minister.
(e) Code of ethics for legislators and civil servants.
(f) Setting up National Judiciary Council to recommend appointment of Judges, lay down ethical framework and empower it to impose minor penalties or recommend removal.
(g) Redefining corruption, collusive bribery and sanction for prosecution.
(h) Corruption by private sector providers of public utility services.
(i) Confiscation of property acquired by illegal means.
(j) Protection of whistle blowers.
(k) Setting up of Lokpal and Lokayuktas.
(l) Protection to legislators and MPs not to cover corrupt act.
(m) Setting up Ombudsman to enquire into corruption in local bodies.
(n) Citizen's charter.
(o) Competition in delivery of public services.
(p) Simplifying methods and procedures.
(q) Using IT.
(r) Integrity pacts
(s) Monitoring of officers.

Individually, several of these are excellent suggestions. One does not see an overarching strategy in the recommendations. A number of these suggestions do not go far enough. The recommendation on ethics commission is only half the step. Violations need to be punished with disqualification from fighting election for periods which the election commission may decide. Similarly a bland suggestion to simplify procedure is not adequate. The institutional mechanism to ensure this is missing. Suggestion on redefining private sector corruption falls short of what other countries are working on.

An Alternative Approach

The reduction of corruption in the country requires a well-integrated strategy. We do not have that. Part of the difficulty has been the reluctance, both among the civil servants and the political executives, to implement reforms. There has been no political consensus on the large-scale changes required to reduce corruption. Several developments in the recent years provide both better consensus and technical ability to make a major diminution possible. We suggest below framework of such a strategy.

The approach to reduce corruption in India should have four dimensions: faster and equitable economic growth, systemic reforms to prevent and minimise corrupt practices, education and community relations with extensive media use to focus on ill effects of corruption, and speedy and independent investigation of corruption cases with expeditious trial of all accused. Extensive use of IT in all the above components should be a key part of the strategy at all levels. Lokpal act has not come into force as appointment of Lokpal has not been notified. Given the past history of opposition to this institution across the entire political spectrum, it is essential that pressure on the government is continuously maintained to set it up quickly.

Economic growth should be the centre piece of any strategy for reducing corruption for several reasons. First, it improves ability of the government to pay more handsome salaries and benefits to their employees. This may reduce their desire for indulging in corrupt practices. A poorly paid civil service is an invitation to corruption. The successful experience of Singapore is a good example.[25]

Second, increased incomes improve the standard of living of population. Both education and health standards improve though may not be proportionately in all cases. The society with an expanding middle class gets more conscious of its rights and starts asking questions. In recent decades, with the increased incomes, accessibility to communication has improved significantly. Newspapers, radio, television and social media can spread positive messages. All these can help develop society's resistance to corruption. The recent movement of Anna Hazare against corruption could gain strength due to strong media support.

Third, growth in incomes cannot take place unless economic policy reforms are implemented. These could include policy for investment of private sector, concession agreements for oil blocks, policy for development of infrastructure, power sector reforms, educational and health sector reforms or similar other reforms, which help the growth process. Generally, economic growth is very strongly related with infrastructure development in these areas. This strengthens domestic capacity to develop new institutions. Such institutions can act as a nucleus and other new institutions of governance can be built on this experience.

Fourth, economic development requires increased private investment. All private investors, while they may put up with inefficiencies and corruption for some time, like to support Rule of Law, especially at grass-roots level where petty corruption is maximum. They, therefore, develop a vested interest in promoting good governance institution.

The experience of global economies supports the above approach. As incomes increase, the ability of country to reduce corruption to a higher level goes up. In low and lower middle income group of countries, there is strong relation between per capita income and level of corruption. Within these groups, one index value reduction in corruption index (on a scale of 0-10) is associated with about $300 increase in average per capita GDP during 1996-2012. The Indian income fall in these group of economies.

All nations have a strong desire to improve the quality of life of their citizens. A focus on economic growth has, hence, a very wide and easy acceptability amongst all classes of population. Everyone is looking for a house, a road in his village connecting to highways, television, motor cycle or car, electricity, a mobile, good quality education and a high level of medical care facilities. These things can come only with economic growth. A focus on growth which has a positive effect on reducing corruption would have huge acceptability in the people.

A criticism has been made in recent debates that economic growth is accompanied by high level of corruption. It has been argued that post-reforms, corruption levels have gone up with increased investments and rise of crony capitalism. There can be no two views on maximising transparency and improving governance to eliminate expansion of crony capitalism. But corruption due to increased investments should be effectively handled too. Level of investment will increase in coming years as we plan for higher growth. The overall strategy must ensure that corruption goes down continuously as a percentage of GDP. Corruption in India has either marginally gone down or remained at the same levels according to perception-based global surveys of the TI and the World Bank. During last two decades, Indian economy has grown at a fast pace with size of GDP increasing by more than five times. Investment in the economy has also increased accordingly.[26] The level of corruption has clearly gone up in terms of dollar value, nature of corrupt acts and its impact across borders. The size of corruption is possibly at the same level in terms of share of GDP. It is a transitional phase. With increase in incomes, corruption levels will start going down not only as a share of GDP but also in absolute value terms as ecosystem improves.

It is difficult to accept for any country that it should stop growing economically because of fear of increased corruption. All studies show that poverty debases human values. There is nothing worse than poverty. All nations with low incomes have a very high level of both petty and political corruption. This needs to be sharply reduced. Experience has shown, and also observed in our analysis, that at about $4,000-5,000 per capita income (at constant 2005 US$) the needs of most of the citizens get satisfied and institutions start getting strong. It is at about this level that corruption is most sensitive to increase in incomes. We are likely to reach these income levels by about 2025-2030 or in another decade. We must focus on economic growth so that our ability to reduce corruption gets strengthened.

Equitable growth requires inclusive growth and sharp reduction in poverty. Large income inequalities create divisions in society. We cannot have two different nations as part of one political entity and hope that there will be no political and economic turmoil. Most nations are, however, finding that recent strategies of growth based on private investment and small public expenditure increase inequality. Consciously, therefore, the nations will have to work towards increased public expenditure on access to education and health services for the poor to increase their capability. Rural infrastructure and policies for positive support to deprived groups will need special attention. This may partly slowdown increasing inequalities. The strategy to reduce corruption by focusing on per capita income increase cannot succeed unless we simultaneously reduce inequality and poverty.

Systemic Reforms

The second component of strategy to fight corruption is systemic reforms. These will need to be worked in two separate areas.

First, we need to address the issue of petty corruption. This requires changing procedures, rules, regulations and laws so that public service delivery is faster. Technology, particularly IT services, and systems like Aadhar Card could be utilised to ensure vastly reduced corruption. Use of IT in procurement and purchase and award of project tenders is important. This is an area of very high corruption potential. A strong political will is required to use IT and make the process transparent. Lot of these reforms are in the ambit of states. Developed economies and many developing economies have been able to change their systems and improve public service delivery. All departments and institutions engaged in public service delivery will need to change their systems and procedures. This will require them to set up units for reforms. The standards of public service delivery must be defined by a citizen's charter and notified. These should be bench marked to global standards.

It should be the responsibility of Lokpal in the centre and Lokayukta in the states to set up advisory bodies within their administrative structure and to monitor and direct progress on systemic reforms. These bodies should work with the departments concerned to improve public service delivery. Each department should be tasked to work with these advisory bodies and install new systems. Since this has already been achieved in many countries, it should not be a problem to use their experience. Within the country too, there is a wide variation in standards of public service delivery. This experience could be utilised. This area of reform would have maximum impact on the citizens.

The Lokpal and Lokayukta should have strong institutional capacity to help government departments and offices to suggest reforms in the above areas. One of the major gaps in the Lokpal Act and Lokayukta Acts as existing in many states is that it has failed to emphasise these areas. The Acts may be amended to provide for it. Second, we need to reduce political corruption or grand corruption or large-scale corruption. This is more difficult to handle and requires basic institutional reforms. Of course, these reforms affect petty corruption too. We mention few key areas of institutional reforms.

The institutions of CAG and CEC, which have performed well and been generally independent in their functioning, need reforms. Both these are key institutions for strengthening democracy and public accountability. The appointment of both CAG and CEC needs to be done by an independent body. ARC has suggested a body, including PM, Leader of Opposition in Lok Sabha, Deputy Chairman of Rajya Sabha, Speaker of Lok Sabha and Law Minister. An independent committee only should appoint both. The suggestion needs to be implemented forthwith.

The major cause of political corruption is human greed and electoral funding. Large expenditure is incurred in elections, funds for which are obtained very often by corrupt means. Further, the number of persons with criminal record coming to the Parliament and state legislatures is very large. Both these areas require reforms. State funding of elections is one alternative. Such funding can be provided to each political party by the state governments (to be provided from Union Budget) based on votes polled in the election held before and some amount based on the membership of the political party. For first time, independent candidates, a similar arrangement based on objective criteria can be developed. This may be criticised on the ground that party or candidate will take the money from the government and spend some more. It may also discriminate against those who join the political stream as a new party and do not have any voters to get this component of funds. Susan Ackerman refers to this dilemma:[27]

> In Germany's strong party state, the Constitutional Court has been specially concerned with the negative impact of public funding on new or small parties. The latest law provides public funding to parties upto an overall ceiling. As a result of the 1992 decision of the Constitutional Court, the new law emphasizes the ability of parties to attract private donations as well as votes. Funds are distributed in proportion to such party's ability to attract both votes and party dues with a formula that disadvantages the longest parties relative to their vote getting power. Contribution from businessmen are permitted but only a portion is to be deductible.

The public funding of election will, however, help lower corruption and ensure greater independence for parties. We could also permit certain press advertisements, television and radio time for the parties in addition to state funding. Norms for this could be developed by election commission. The public funding of election will result in lower corruption and ensure greater independence in policy making for parties. We should start this initially with few by-elections and then expand it.

An important factor determining political corruption is nature of candidates fighting elections. Candidates with criminal background need to be debarred from elections. The law laid down by the Supreme Court that candidates convicted of serious offences should be debarred from fighting elections is a good beginning. This should form the starting point. For future, stricter guidelines could be developed by election commission. All cases where charge sheets have been filed, offences are of serious nature, and courts have taken cognisance of the case should attract debarment of candidates. The deterrence on candidates with criminal record can only be effective if cases are tried speedily and punishment handed out quickly. Judgments in cases of former ministers Sukh Ram and Lalu Prasad Yadav took more than a decade. The Supreme Court and the High Courts must set up special court for this. These courts, to be termed High-level Anti-Corruption courts, should be set up in all states. Unfortunately, there has been slow progress in setting up courts.

Rule of evidence involving use of IT, permitting e-filing and fixing time-limits for tendering evidence by defence or by prosecution should be prescribed by law. Such courts should take only class A and class B officers, ministers, MPs and large value political corruption cases to ensure quick decision and trial.

Women can play a very important role in reducing corruption. Studies have confirmed that women are less corrupt as compared to men.[28] Their participation as MP or MLA has so far been about 10-11 per cent and has remained roughly at this level. All political parties, through an amendment in the electoral law, must be required to have at least 50 per cent women contestants in all elections. This will ensure sufficient number of them getting elected. A party should be permitted to contest elections (state legislature as well as Parliament) only if sufficient number of women candidates participate. Over the next 15 years, we should plan for at least one-third women MPs and state legislatures.[29]

Ethical Values

Adoption of ethical values is a key policy intervention for preventing corruption. Civil servants, ministers, MPs and other elected representatives must be asked to follow certain ethical values and declare their financial assets every year which should be put on the website. Already there is a code of conduct for central ministers. This needs to be reviewed and brought in line with low corruption developed economies. It is essential that we have in each state a body of 10-15 investigators working under Lokpal whose job should be to constantly monitor the financial returns and report to Election Commission or the Lokpal corrupt behaviour or movement towards it. In addition to above, adherence to ethical norms should also be monitored by an institutional mechanism set up by the PM, an Independent Commission on Ethics and the Ethics Committees of two Houses. In addition to above, the Lokpal and Lokayukta through their own agency should also monitor implementation of ethical code by public servants. An important ethical value, which must be a part of the ethics code, is the Conflict of Interest. In any such case, the official or Minister should recuse himself from the case. Violation of such values must be punished with warnings or disability to fight elections, apart from criminal action depending on seriousness of the violation.

Acceptance of gifts by public officials is another area which is very worrisome in the Indian context. S.S. Gill (1998) talks of *nazrana*, *shukrana* and *jabrana* in the Mughal times.[30] In the British Raj, it became a tradition for officials to offer and accept gifts. Halayya (1985) talks of costly gifts or presents being accepted by the departing British officers.[31] The corrupt tradition has continued even after Independence. In fact, in our experience, it has expanded enormously with any festive occasion being used to give gifts. A time has come to put a stop to it. Such gifts are taboo in some countries and in some others permitted with a lot of safeguards. Except for non-value gifts like memento with no commercial value, all gifts from persons with whom one has any official dealings or any official relation should be banned. Exception could be made for gifts on ceremonial occasions. All such gifts should be returned to the government and donated for charitable causes or kept for record. This would promote a culture of simplicity and honest dealings.

Community Values and Education

The third component of anti-corruption strategy is community education. Societies have widely varying moral values. Lot of these depend upon the customs, traditions and development over the centuries. It is possible to bring changes in these through education and public discourse by opinion leaders and intellectuals. A successful example is the strong opposition to smoking all over the world after a sustained campaign against smoking.

Corruption is a cancer-like phenomenon and ought to be addressed accordingly. A very extensive system of media campaign against corruption is needed. This should include community education and extensive discussions with different opinion making groups. The responsibility for managing this should be taken by Lokpal and Lokayukta and be fully backed by the government. These communication experts should give messages through lectures in offices, in schools, on the television and radio and also through the press. The whole exercise has to be done as a national campaign and backed by the 'advisory groups' set up by them to get ideas and people's participation.

Investigation, Trial and Punishment of the Corrupt

While impact of systemic reforms, community education and economic growth on corruption reduction is positive, independent investigation, speedy trial and punishment of the guilty and corrupt public servant, howsoever high in civil and political circles, are absolutely essential for controlling corruption. A strong political will is essential for this. It is very difficult to develop it in most countries.

To ensure this in the political environment prevailing in the country which is characterised by lack of intellectual integrity, we needed an independent and credible institution. The Lokpal fills this requirement to a very great extent. To ensure complete independence in investigation of all cases of corruption and ensure a well-coordinated approach on fighting corruption, it is essential that CBI and CVC are brought under Lokpal. Under the current Lokpal Act, this is contemplated in most areas. It however still leaves gaps which may diminish independence of investigating agency. Let us mention some areas of reform.

First, in cases where tenure of an investigating officer is over and he is not working on a case sent to CBI by Lokpal, central government may send repatriation orders to exercise influence. This may be especially so where the government is unhappy with the way an investigation is progressing.

Second, most of the senior officers in CBI come from state governments and are part of force under control of the central government. They revert back to states after a fixed tenure. To expect that they will not be influenced by powerful politicians with connections is not reasonable.

Third, there is a lack of clarity on functioning of the system. The CBI will be, as part of its normal responsibilities, registering cases and conducting investigations. Another class of cases will be those which will be sent by Lokpal. This will not be conducive to independent functioning of CBI. The government may ask for details or exercise influence over cases registered by CBI of its own.

Fourth, supervision of the CVC or Lokpal over CBI investigation will not mean much unless Lokpal can direct inclusion or deletion of name of any accused based on assessment of evidence. The supervision may otherwise be in the nature of progress report. That will not serve any purpose. The Lokpal should have complete power to direct investigation. To ensure fairness, a check of independent nature is essential.

Fifth, the Lokpal should gradually build its own cadre and the part of bureau left outside Lokpal should deal only with criminal cases excluding corruption. All cases of corruption should only be dealt with by them and CVC. The independence of Lokpal cadre will ensure independent investigation without influence of powerful politicians or civil servants. While the anti-corruption wing of CBI may form the initial investigation team on corruption cases under the Lokpal, the question of how such an investigation agency is recruited later is an important one. Independence of people who form part of it is important. In Singapore, such an agency recruited people independently and did not get them from the existing police force. While many officers of CBI are of the highest level of integrity, as a policy it would be necessary to have the institution's recruitment from independent sources. The Lokpal should build its own investigative wing. They could train these people well. On a long-term basis, they cannot depend upon other agencies. People who join it should be a permanent part of the institution. The independence and integrity of personnel is of highest importance.

Sixth, there should be a time limit fixed for the government and charged officers to give their response to Lokpal before it makes up its mind on permitting or not permitting prosecution. Similarly, while time limit of 90 days is prescribed to get enquiries completed, it is not clear what would happen if the enquiry remains incomplete after the above period. Necessary provisions must be made to ensure speedy enquiries.

The Lokpal should be concerned primarily with ministers, MPs, senior public servants and all Class A and Class B officers. The rest should be looked by CVC. Even now the scheme of thing is that CVC will take a decision about this group. This will ensure that big cases do not go scot-free or investigation delayed due to pressure of work. This is a good approach and should not be diluted.

An important area of concern is the press leaks of investigation being done by CBI. The investigation, while being fair, should not be conducted with bulletins to the media on day-to-day basis. Most countries conduct these investigations quickly and confidentially. Since in many cases, trial takes time and investigations prolong in India, system of trial by media especially on television channels exists. Information available in all these cases is not complete as investigations are generally ongoing. This is neither fair to the state nor the accused. The punishment by way of loss of public image and sullying of the name gets inflicted immediately. Possibly the system has evolved as regular investigation and trial takes very long and the investigating agencies are in a hurry to show some effective action. This is not part of a healthy tradition. All investigations must be done quickly until the case goes to the court.

In many countries including the US and Hong Kong, the investigation of cases on corruption is done by independent investigation agencies, but prosecution and decision about it is taken by the government. In the US, for some time, there was a system of special prosecutors under a law which had a sunset clause. A decision on this is now taken by the Attorney General. If both investigation and decision on prosecution itself are taken by the Lokpal, there is possibility of misuse of authority due to excessive concentration of powers. To ensure checks and balance, the decisions on prosecution in court should be taken by the government. For prosecution of such cases in the court, a panel of special prosecutors may be prepared on the recommendation of Attorney General and approved by the Lokpal. After investigation of a case is over and Lokpal is satisfied that a *prima facie* case of corruption is made out, it will sanction the prosecution after considering all facts including view point of the government. The charge sheet may then be sent to special prosecutor for filing in court. If there are concerns, he will take up with the investigative officer of Lokpal. The check will ensure a balance of power and a fair investigation not influenced by the government in power.

The persons working with Lokpal will be drawn from our society in which so much corruption exists. There conduct may reflect this. It will be appropriate for Lokpal to set up a separate wing to monitor corrupt employees of Lokpal. A very close watch and fast punishment to the guilty will act as a deterrent.

The Lokayukta Act should have provisions similar to those of Lokpal Act. In the state, the Anti-Corruption Wing of the police should be under the Lokayukta. The independence of investigation cannot be ensured by half-hearted measures. Such a body on anti-corruption issues should be outside the influence of government. The above arrangement would ensure this. Over the years, recruitment to this body should be done independently by the Lokayukta itself. It should have a small prosecution wing. The Advocate General (AG) or Special Counsel approved by Lokayukta on recommendation of AG should prosecute the cases in court by a procedure similar to the one adopted by Lokpal. In case of difference of view, the Lokayukta will decide on prosecution or otherwise. In all such cases, the views of Attorney General or of Special Counsel would be available both to the Lokayukta and the court to which the result of investigation goes for decision on closure of case or going ahead with trial.

An independent selection of Lokayukta by a Committee similar to that of the centre and its approval by Governor would be necessary to ensure a truly independent office. The Lokayukta police have been quite effective in Karnataka and Madhya Pradesh. Once the anti-corruption wing comes under Lokayukta, it could, based on information, carry out search and seizure operations.

Two drivers of anti-corruption efforts are fair and independent investigation and speedy trial. Global experience is that grand corruption or political corruption in most of the economies is quite large. However, they have a system of independent investigation and speedy trial. The Lokpal Act does not fully address the issue of speedy trial. There is a need to have notified Special Anti-Corruption Courts, which should deal with these cases. One could have two streams: courts dealing with cases of corruption of senior civil servants, Ministers, MPs, MLAs and other Group 'A' and Group 'B' officers. The other class of Courts could handle Group 'C' and Group 'D' corruption cases. Both the High Court and the Supreme Court need to agree to this system and the state government should quickly set them up. Trials in these cases should be done expeditiously. Unless this aspect of anti-corruption effort is looked at, no impact on corruption would be felt.

As incomes in the Indian economy rise, inclusive growth expands. The other three components of anti-corruption strategy should simultaneously be implemented along with use of modern technology at all stages. We can become, in 2030, a society with very high level of integrity and honesty. This would reinforce economic growth and provide a vastly improved quality of life to the citizens.

Notes and References

1. The *Arthashastra* is an ancient Indian treatise on statecraft, economic policy and military strategy, written in Sanskrit. It identifies its author by the names Kautilya and Vishnugupta—both names that are traditionally identified with Chanakya (c.350–283 BC), who was a scholar at Takshashila and the teacher and guardian of Emperor Chandragupta Maurya, founder of the Mauryan Empire. The text was influential until the 12th century, when it disappeared. It was rediscovered in 1904 by R. Shamasastry, who published it in 1909. The first English translation was published in 1915.
2. Kangle, R.P. (1965). *The Kautiliya Arthashastra* (Part I-III). New Delhi: Motilal Banarsidas Publishers. . In his commentary of translation of *Arthashastra*, Kangle observes that he has used several manuscripts of *Arthashastra* while preparing the final version. Also, the work does not consider morally or ethically undesirable actions, if they are in actual practice resorted to in the supreme interest of the state (Vol. Part-III: 264-65).
3. East India Company was given the right to trade in early 19th century. In the initial years, the employees of the company had very low salaries and were allowed to trade their own benefit. They misused the exemption given by the Nawabs and local governments and indulged in massive corruption. The salaries of the East India Company officials were so low in the mid-1700s—£5 annually for a writer (an apprentice), £15 for a factor, £30 for a junior merchant—that impecunity invited company personnel to augment their incomes by engaging in private trade within India. The tradition of corruption can be traced to Robert Clive, victor of the Battle of Plassey (1757), on whom the grateful Nawab of Bengal bestowed the military rank of Jagir, which brought with it a stipend derived from land taxes. Clive returned to England with £300,000 and an additional £28,000 a year. See also: Burroughs, Catherine (ed.) (2000). *Women in British Romantic Theatre: Drama, Performance and Society, 1790-1840*. Cambridge University Press.
4. *http://parliamentofindia.nic.in/ls/debates/vol11p12.htm* (accessed on 24 August 2014).
5. Ibid.
6. Myrdal, Gunnar (1968). *Asian Drama: An Inquiry into the Poverty of Nations*. 3 Vols. Allen Lane: The Penguin Press.
7. *http://rbidocs.rbi.org.in/rdocs/content/PDFs/90045.pdf* (accessed on 2 September 2014).
8. Gill, S.S. (1998). *The Pathology of Corruption*. New Delhi: Harper Collins.

9. *Economic Survey, 2013-14*, available at: *http://indiabudget.nic.in/survey.asp*
10. For more details than provided here, please refer to reports of CAG Report on 2G Spectrum and another report on coal-blocks allocation. The Judicial proceedings is a matter of public records.
11. CAG Report No.7 of 2012-13 for the period ended March 2012: Performance Audit of Allocation of Coal Blocks and Augmentation of Coal Production (Ministry of Coal), available at: *www.cag.gov.in*
12. TI has published the CPI annually ranking countries "by their perceived levels of corruption, as determined by expert assessments and opinion surveys." Based on a long-standing research programme of the World Bank, the Worldwide Governance Indicators capture six key dimensions of governance (voice and accountability, political stability and lack of violence, government effectiveness, regulatory quality, rule of law and control of corruption) between 1996 and present. They measure the quality of governance in over 200 countries, based on close to 40 data sources produced by over 30 organisations worldwide and are updated annually since 2002.
13. *World Bank Development Indicator, 2012,* available at: *http://data.worldbank.org/data-catalog/world-development-indicators*
14. Wade, Robert (1982). "Corruption: Where Does the Money Go?", *Economic and Political Weekly* 37(40).
15. Debroy, B. and L. Bhandari (2012). *Corruption in India: The DNA and RNA*. Konark Publications. pp.162-63.
16. In June 2005, TI India released its India Corruption Study 2005, undertaken in alliance with the CMS, Delhi. The "India Corruption Study 2005" is the largest corruption study ever undertaken in the country with a sample of 14,405 respondents spread across 20 States. More than 525 respondents were interviewed in each state. Designed and conducted by CMS, the study covered 151 cities and 306 villages. It was based on a combination of research methodologies, including exit polls at the public offices covered and household studies. It's available at: *http://archive.transparency.org/regional_pages/asia_pacific/newsroom/news_archive2/india_corruption_study_2005* (accessed on 3 September 2014)
17. Debroy, B. and L. Bhandari (2012). *Corruption in India: The DNA and RNA*. Konark Publications. pp.162-63.
18. E&Y (2013). Survey on Bribery and Corruption: Ground Reality in India. Available at: *http://www.ey.com/Publication/vwLUAssets/Bribery_and_corruption:_ground_reality_in_India/$FILE/EY-FIDS-Bribery-and-corruption-ground-reality-in-India.pdf* (accessed on Sep 6, 2014).
19. KPMG (2011). *Survey on Bribery and Corruption: Impact on Economy and Business Environment.* Available at: *http://www.kpmg.com/IN/en/IssuesAndInsights/ThoughtLeadership/KPMG_Bribery_Survey_Report_new.pdf* (accessed on Sep 6, 2014).
20. Halayya, M. (1985). *Corruption in India.* New Delhi: Affiliated East-West Press.
21. *http://www.financialtransparency.org/2010/08/16/illicit-financial-flows-from-developing-countries-the-absurdity-of-traditional-methods-of-estimation/* (accessed on Sep 3, 2014)
22. Russell, Jenniffer (2012). "E-Governance and Corruption in the States: Can Technology Help the Aam Admi", *Economic & Political Weekly* XIVII(25): 77. See also: The Ministry of Corporate Affairs (MCA), Government of India, has initiated the MCA-21 project, which enables easy and secure access to MCA services in an assisted manner for corporate entities, professionals and general public. The MCA-21 project is designed to fully automate all processes related to enforcement and compliance of the legal requirements under the Companies Act, 1956. The project further seeks to achieve inter-operability with the National e-Governance Services

Delivery Gateway (NSDG), which will help extend MCA services to businesses *via* multiple front-end delivery channels, and which will also help provide other value-added services over and above the base services offered by MCA21.

23. PMGSY was launched on 25 December 2000 as a fully funded Centrally Sponsored Scheme to provide all weather road connectivity in rural areas of the country. The programme envisages connecting all habitations with a population of 500 persons and above in the plain areas and 250 persons and above in hill States, the tribal and the desert areas. Details available at: *www.pmgsy.nic.in*

24. The Administrative Reforms Commission or ARC is the committee appointed by the Government of India for giving recommendations for reviewing the public administrative system of India.The Second ARC was constituted on 31 August 2005, as a Commission of Inquiry, under the Chairmanship of Veerappa Moily for preparing a detailed blueprint for revamping the public administrative system. The Commission was given the mandate to suggest measures to achieve a proactive, responsive, accountable, sustainable and efficient administration for the country at all levels of the government. The Commission was asked to, inter alia, consider the following: (i) organisational structure of the GoI, (ii) ethics in governance, (iii) refurbishing of personnel administration, (iv) strengthening of financial management systems, (v) steps to ensure effective administration at the state level, (vi) steps to ensure effective district administration, (vii) local self-government/panchayati raj institutions, (viii) social capital, trust and participative public service delivery, (ix) citizen-centric administration, (x) promoting e-governance, (xi) issues of federal polity, (xii) crisis management and (xiii) public order.

25. Rijckeghem, Caroline Van and Beatrice Weder (1997). "Corruption and the Rate of Temptation: Do Low Wages in the Civil Service Cause Corruption?", *IMF Working Paper.* Available at: *http://www.imf.org/external/pubs/ft/wp/wp9773.pdf* (Accessed on Sept. 3, 2014).

26. *World Bank Development Indicator, 2012*, available at: *http://data.worldbank.org/data-catalog/world-development-indicators*

27. Ackerman, Susan R. (1999). *Corruption and Government: Causes Consequences and Reforms.* Cambridge University Press.

28. Swamy, A., Stephen Knack, Y. Lee and Omar Azfar (2000). "Gender and Corruption", *CDE Working Paper Series.* MA, USA: Centre for Development Economics, Williams College. See also: Dollar, David, Raymond Fisman and Roberta Gatti (2001). "Are Women Really the Fairer Sex? Corruption and Women in Government",*Journal of Economic Behavior & Organization* 46(4): 423-29.

29. Agarwal, U.C. (2011). "Corruption Prevention: Need for Effective and Rational Approach", *Indian Journal of Public Administration* 57: 381-82.

30. Gill, S.S. (1998). *The Pathology of Corruption.* New Delhi: Harper Collins.

31. Halayya, M. (1985). *Corruption in India.* New Delhi: Affiliated East-West Press.

7

Conclusion

In recent years corruption has become a part of public debate both within nations and in international discourse. The growing concern highlights its moral and economic dimension. Corrupt societies have large inbuilt tensions. If in the normal life of people they are not sure whether statements made by other persons are trustworthy, society will be busy guarding itself against possible risks. No worthwhile business can be transacted in such situations. If incomes and benefits from the government, which are due to you under rules, are appropriated by someone else because he has better connections or due to bribes being taken by officials or politicians, orderly society gets weakened. If common people feel that the ruling political class or senior civil servants are collecting taxes and putting large sums of money in their banks, a revolution is sooner or later going to engulf the nation. Corrupt politicians in many countries are misusing funds received from the World Bank at soft interest rates or siphoning off money from aid-projects, adversely affecting beneficiaries. In international business, several firms won contracts by paying bribes to politicians. This resulted in unfair terms of trade. It was realised that corruption breeds inefficiencies and thus impacts growth. These concerns have put the issue of corruption in the middle of public discourse.[1]

Corruption and Ethics

Corruption, in the context of humans, implies 'dishonest or fraudulent conduct'. It signifies moral depravity, moral debasement or lowering of moral stature. In the context of public officials, it indicates 'misuse of public office for private gain'. Corrupt actions involve acts of commission and also of omission. The term has implications for private institutions or organisations like firms, companies, stock exchanges or such other entities. The meaning of the term has several grey areas. In many societies, giving gift and accepting it is a part of societal custom and values. In others, it is clearly not part of their tradition. Several actions though corrupt in sense of getting unfair advantage are not necessarily illegal. Benefits resulting from networking with peers and clients, maintaining close contact with powerful politicians or using your school connection to obtain a good placement for your son fall in this category. While framing our laws on corruption, we should apply the norm whether certain actions lower the confidence of people in the fairness of government system or not. The real test in case of public acts of officials should be whether personal gain has accrued or is expected or was attempted by a public official. Unless a nexus is there, merely because certain act was done or delayed, is not sufficient to call the act corrupt. Distinction between bona fide mistake, negligence and corrupt act is important. Bribe-giver and the public official accepting it should normally be considered guilty of corrupt acts. The culpability of bribe-giver arises as he corrupts the institution and lowers the moral standard of public official. He cannot be looked at as a mere victim. In a private entity, the concept of corruption should also include private gain from corrupt acts of an agent against the wishes of the principal.

Corrupt acts also raise questions of ethical values. The offering of bribe to government dispensary to get a medicine outside working hours to save a child's life is a corrupt act but may not be unethical. Offering bribes to a public official to expedite clearance of a drinking water project which will save hundreds of life is corrupt but may not be called an unethical act by many as far as bribe-giver is concerned. In the Second World War, there were hundreds of lives saved due to bribing of Nazi officials. In a repressive regime, giving bribe to save life of a popular leader may be illegal and corrupt act but may not be considered unethical by the people. Evaluating the worth of an action in ethical terms when the act is corrupt in terms of a law is a difficult task. The great German philosopher Immanuel Kant would regard action as moral if it is in conformity with a duty. He would consider consequences of an action as irrelevant for the moral worth of an action. Mahatma Gandhi would emphasise purity of means. *Bhagwat Gita* talks of performance of Dharma, irrespective of the consequences. These questions arise during actual prosecution of cases and have no easy answers. The concept of corruption should include private gain from public office and corrupt acts of an agent, in a private entity, against wishes of the principal.

Definition of Corruption and its Measurement

The definition of corruption under the laws on corruption of different countries has been generally expanded to include corruption in government organisations and in private companies. The United Nations Development Programme (UNDP) definition had earlier considered corruption as "misuse of public power, office or authority for private benefit through bribery, extortion, influence paddling, nepotism, fraud, speed money or embezzlement." It has now been expanded to "misuse of entrusted power for private gain" to signify inclusion of corruption in private companies. In Singapore, Hong Kong, the US and India, it includes advantages of any nature both pecuniary and non-pecuniary. It also covers acts of commission or omission. The benefits received or expected or to be received by public servant are in such cases an inducement to do or abstain from doing an official act.[2]

Several other features of corruption law are common in the above countries. The definition of public servants is fairly wide and covers all organisations where a public duty is being performed. It covers Members of Parliament (MPs), ministers and all officials. The bribe-givers as well as the official taking the bribe are equally liable for punishment. In India, however, the bribe-giver is punishable only as an abettor but not as an equally liable person.[3] Under a specific provision under our corruption law, statements made by bribe-giver cannot be used against him. Under the UN Convention against Corruption (UNCAC), such liability is in equal measure on both. The Indian law needs to be changed on this count. In the laws on corruption in the above countries, if any benefit is received by any official, the onus of proof that such gratification or benefit has been received legally is on him. It is the charged official who has to prove that it was received in accordance with rules and presumption is against him. Corruption in private companies is punishable in Hong Kong and Singapore. In India, the Administrative Reforms Commission (ARC) did not recommend change in Indian Law. The provisions in the Companies Act cannot serve the purpose of corruption law and this need to be amended to cover corruption in private companies.

The law on corruption in India needs to change in another area. The provision on criminal misconduct under section 13(1)(d)(iii) is very open ended and 'private gain', a key element of the law in all countries is missing. It also leaves doors wide open on the definition of the word 'public interest'. These provisions inhibit risk taking and provide no protection to bona fide acts of civil servants. This needs to be amended or scrapped.

Measurement of corruption requires indices which are available to all researchers and also fairly broad based. The Corruption Indices of the Transparency International (TI) and the World Bank are in public domain and are available to all. It is, however, based on perception of different organisations and averaged out to get more realistic assessment. In spite of the limitation, these are used for analysis. To this extent, results are more of indicative nature.

Petty Corruption and Political Corruption

The nature of corruption globally includes petty corruption and political corruption. The main driver of petty corruption is the civil servants. It involves delivery of services at grass-roots level. Some of these are: getting ration cards, electric connection, driving licence, passport, caste certificate, registration of a case in police station, fighting a case in court and similar other services. The main beneficiary in such cases is the official with some share of politicians too. Political corruption is large-scale corruption where the main drivers are generally politicians. In several cases, these are also senior business executives. Such cases of corruption are involved in major contracts, concessions, large value purchases and tenders. While petty corruption is very low in developed countries, it has large presence in developing economies. It impacts the life of most citizens in these countries and leads to huge inefficiencies. Political corruption erodes the confidence of people in the government and destabilises it. Political corruption is very difficult to fight. However, unless this is done, the ecosystem in society will remain weak on corruption.

Corruption and Growth

Corruption has very significantly impacted economies across the globe in terms of their GDP (gross domestic product) growth and per capita incomes. Nearly 55 per cent of the countries have high level of corruption. There are two diverse views on influence of corruption on GDP growth. A body of thinkers and economists argue that corruption reduces growth by dis-incentivising investment in the economy. Cost of project goes up with payment of bribes. The quantum of bribes required to be paid being uncertain, computing of project viability is often difficult. During the implementation of the project, more bribes may have to be paid to get clearances, for smooth operation, and on compliance of local laws. Labour inspector or urban development authority may ask for money on a regular basis to give various certificates and clearances. Investor/s may be threatened with cancellation of allotted coal mines or environment clearances given earlier, or new ministers opening up all project approvals given by an earlier government. Additional bribes may have to be paid to avoid this. Investor also runs the risk of violation of integrity clauses being included in terms of contract after the UNCAC has come into force, leading to cancellation of orders and future adverse consequences. The quality of infrastructure is often very poor due to corruption. This leads to inefficiencies in the economy and higher output costs.

An alternate view on impact of corruption is that it supports higher investments and growth. Bribes act as an incentive to get faster clearances. It helps reducing project delays. By bribing ministers and officials, investments fructify quickly. This lowers the cost of project. During execution of project, payment of bribes keeps the officials interested and improves efficiency. In countries with large natural resources, bribes enable securing of contract without delay leading to faster exploitation of natural resources. In absence of bribes, decisions are delayed adversely impacting GDP growth. In countries with low protection of property rights, corruption ensures smoother functioning.

Cross-country Study

Cross-country study for 67 countries was done by Mauro (1995) for the period 1960-1985. He concluded that corruption impacted investment/GDP adversely. Using a data source of Business International (BI), he concluded that one standard deviation decrease in corruption index resulted in lower investment/GDP of 2.23 per cent. Subsequent authors using TI data concluded that the negative impact on GDP growth per annum may vary from 0.13 to 0.50 per cent for one index value change in corruption index. For several major economies with high level of corruption, the total impact may be 2 per cent if corruption were to be eliminated completely. Similar calculations were made for per capita incomes by Dreher and Herzfeld (2005) who computed that net impact of corruption in increasing per capita income was $445 for one index value lower corruption.[4]

Our analysis using World Bank data for 147 countries for the period 1996-2012 indicates that corruption lowers growth but in several economies it had a positive impact too. Our results indicated that investment/GDP growth in African economies was severely affected by corruption. An increased corruption by one index value (on a scale of 0-10) led to 0.90 per cent of higher investment/GDP. However in Asian economies, it lowered investment by 0.83 per cent for similar increase in corruption. In remaining economies, it lowered investment with developed economies showing little impact. In these countries, corruption is not an issue as most of them already have low level of corruption. Investment in these countries is dependent on other factors.

GDP growth during the above period according to our analysis was lower by 0.36 per cent with if corruption increased by one index value. Its impact was high in low income economies. In these economies, increase in corruption by one index value reduced growth by 0.49 per cent. In lower middle income economies, in which India also is included, the impact was higher with one index value increased corruption levels lowering growth by 0.73 per cent. There was thus a very sharp decline in growth with increased corruption in this income range. In upper middle income countries, the increased corruption levels of one index value led to lowering of growth rates by 0.30 per cent. In high income countries, the impact was very small as most of them have already very low level of corruption. The impact of corruption on growth is dependent very significantly on income levels of economies.

We also studied the impact of corruption on other factors on which GDP growth depends. After accounting for impact of corruption on these factors, we estimated the total (both direct and indirect) impact of one index value change in corruption index on GDP growth at 0.40 per cent point, up from 0.36 per cent point in case of direct impact of corruption alone.

Our estimate of the impact of corruption on per capita GDP in 147 countries for the period 1996-2012 indicates an increase in income of $304 due to lowering of corruption levels by one index value on a scale of 0-10. The impact was highest in lower middle income countries at $329. Since most of high income group countries already have very low level of corruption, the change in per capita income in the group was very small. We estimate that for all economies together after accounting for indirect impact of corruption on other factors, the net (both direct and indirect) impact would be an increase of $450 in GDP per capita for one index value lower corruption. If India were to have lower corruption similar to Scandinavian economies since 1996 and were to maintain it at that level, our average per capita incomes during 1996-2012 would be three times of current levels and GDP growth would be about 2 per cent higher.

Factors Impacting Corruption

The rate of economic growth of a country is determined by several factors including corruption. The degree of corruption within the nations is, however, determined by a number of elements some of which are an outcome of economic growth. Factors determining corruption in a country include per capita incomes, poverty, inequalities in incomes, investments in the economy, government expenditure, political stability, voice and accountability, education specially at secondary school level, nature of the society, and quality of institutions of governance. Each of these factors exhibit interesting features.

Corruption shows practically no relation with investment/GDP. In some income groups, there is indication that corruption may be impacted. This is determined by local political conditions or some societal factor. There is, however, no trend. In individual countries, investment may be a significant factor. It is particularly so in African economies. Unlike investment, government expenditure impacts corruption. The largest impact is at low income levels. In all income groups, increase in government expenditure helps reduce corruption. The public expenditure helps in the process of economic growth, and larger investment in infrastructure, education and health. These help reduce corruption.

Higher per capita incomes help lowering of corruption. At low or low middle income levels, this impact is not significant. At these income levels corruption is determined by other factors. Higher incomes and growth provide an ecosystem conducive to lowering of corruption. With income levels of above $4,000 the per capita incomes help in lowering of corruption levels and development of an ecosystem which facilitates this process. At higher incomes, the opposition to corrupt acts of public servants from the people is stronger. Government officials are paid well and they have lesser inclination for taking bribes.

Both political stability and voice and accountability have an impact on corruption. At all income levels, political stability has a significant positive impact and is conducive to lowering of corruption. It reduces the risk which any investment entails. Political stability is indicative of stable government regime. In countries which are under autocratic regimes or under dictators, this may not be so. Voice and accountability has very little impact on corruption in low income economies. The institutions of political governance are better organised at higher income levels. This is reflected in a weaker explanatory significance of these variables at lower incomes.

Secondary school education influences employability of citizens, and ability of society for public discourse on issues of corruption. Primary education is now well organised in most of these countries. Boys and girls of the 6-14 years age group are in schools. It is not so with secondary schools. Analysis indicates that once the society has

90 per cent of target population in schools, the corruption in society is impacted. A highly literate society is conscious of its rights. It is likely to help lower corruption. In most of high income countries, secondary school education enrolment levels are more than 90 per cent.

Both inequalities in incomes and levels of poverty increase corruption. Available data for about 60 countries show that both of these indicators influence corruption levels. High inequality creates division in society. Poverty adversely impacts quality of life. It induces and incentivises corrupt behaviour especially in societies with wide income and consumption disparity.

The nature of society, especially if it consists of different ethnic, racial and religious or other close-knit social groups, provides an ecosystem conducive to high level corruption. This fractionalisation of society results in groups which tend to be indulgent to their members even when violation of law is clearly made out.

Corruption is most strongly influenced by institutions of governance and quality of their functioning. Rule of law, regulatory structure and effectiveness of the government depends upon how well the institutions are organised, independence given to them for functioning, and quality of people managing them. Both police and judiciary are two basic components of this structure. If corruption level or inefficiencies in these are high, its impact multiplies several folds in other areas. The economic regulations and their management is another critical field influencing corruption. The independence of audit institutions and government's serious response to their observations strengthens faith of investors in governance system of the country.

International Experience

International experience shows that global society has been concerned with increasing corruption. UNCAC has been signed and ratified by 171 countries till April 2014. The convention sets out various provisions for controlling corruption to which the signatories agree. These include cooperation with each other in fighting corruption, assistance in recovery of proceeds of corrupt acts and establishment of anti-corruption bodies. The convention comprehensively mentions various others ideas on transparency in financing of election campaign and laws on corrupt acts including those committed in private companies.

Experiences of several countries like Finland, the US, Singapore and Hong Kong show that control of corruption is strongly influenced by per capita incomes, independence of anti-corruption institutions, quality of the civil service and its code of ethics, transparency in the system and community education. The experience of the US, Brazil and Italy shows that political corruption is prevalent in all economies and is most difficult to eliminate. The major cause of political corruption is financing of elections. Corruption in private businesses has also expanded significantly over the years with increasing competition amongst different manufacturing and trading companies. The US law, Foreign Corruption Prevention Act (FCPA) 1977 has taken a very major initiative by declaring bribing of public officials or other persons an illegal act. It is applicable to foreign citizens and companies working in the US. Most of the countries have now set up anti-corruption agencies. The critical part of removing corruption is a strong political will and speedy trials of offenders. Global experience shows that prevention of corruption, educating people about it, developing community relations and effective implementation of laws on bribery are important, while high level of incomes create a good ecosystem for reducing corruption. Singapore has successfully handled this by giving very high salaries to civil servants and political executives.

Incomes, Ecosystem and Corruption Boundary

Strategy for fighting corruption has to consider economic growth as a key component. Global experience shows that group of countries with low incomes have very high level of corruption. Of this group, 96.8 per cent have Corruption Perceptions Index (CPI) score of less than 5.0 and 54.8 per cent of them have CPI score of 3.0 or below. The countries in this group are not able to reach a level of low corruption which is signified by a score of 7.0 on CPI scales. Thus, the low per capita incomes act as a boundary condition and create an ecosystem which restricts large reduction in corruption. As incomes rise, these boundaries expand. In countries with lower middle incomes and upper middle income, the percentage of countries with low corruption perception index of less than 3.0 goes down to 40.0 per cent and 17.1 per cent against 54.8 per cent of low income countries. Simultaneously, the share of countries with CPI scores between 3.0 and 5.0 increases to 65.7 per cent, 54.3 per cent and 41.9 per cent respectively for different income groups. Thus, with increase of incomes, share of countries with different corruption level keeps on going up.

As incomes go up further, the boundary keeps on expanding and 46.8 per cent of the countries in high income group have CPI more than 7.0. Also, 31.9 per cent have CPI scores in the range of 5.0 to 7.0 as against 17.1 per cent, 5.7 per cent and 3.2 per cent respectively for lower income groups. Higher the income, higher is the boundary up to which countries in an income group can reduce corruption due to improved ecosystem. The ecosystem reflects the environment in the society due to higher incomes, quality of health and education particularly of secondary stage, inequalities in income and poverty levels and health of governance institutions. Higher incomes generally provide an improved ecosystem and an expanding boundary.

Fighting Corruption

The strategy for fighting corruption has to be anchored on increasing incomes. This will require larger investments. There are concerns that higher investment may mean higher corruption. In a cross-country analysis, investment as a share of GDP has been found to have very little correlation with corruption. The corruption perception index of countries like China and India, which had large investment in the last two decades, is almost stable. It is, however, clear that with increase in size of the economies by 3 to 10 times in Brazil, Malaysia, India and China, the corruption has increased in terms of dollars. As a share of GDP, there is no evidence that it has increased.[5] Considering increasing size of GDPs, across the world and particularly in developing countries, the corruption may have increased in dollar value terms and can adopt different forms in coming years. We need a strong fight against corruption based on larger incomes and improving ecosystem.

Global experience shows that during 1996-2012, countries which reduced corruption by highest margins included Georgia, Rwanda, Liberia, Estonia, Latvia, Croatia and Serbia apart from others. All these countries increased their GDP by margins much higher than the global average. As against this, countries like Côte d'Ivoire, Eritrea, Zimbabwe, South Africa, Yemen Republic, Fiji and Kuwait had the worst performance in terms of CPI. All these countries reduced their GDP or grew at a lower rate than the global average. In the top 10 countries, which had highest levels of worsening of corruption during 1996-2012, only Trinidad and Tobago and Turkmenistan had increased incomes. This is consistent with the view that increase in incomes plays a major role in reducing corruption.

The strategy to reduce corruption must be built around economic growth. It must, however, have a comprehensive approach and include in it prevention of corruption which involves easy procedures, simpler laws and regulations, use of technology, participation of community and a strong and effective implementation of laws. The development of institutions of governance is the foundation for such reduction. The strategy for fighting corruption has to consider all these factors to succeed.

Corruption in India

Corruption in governance in India has been discussed in *Arthashastra* where Chanakya has mentioned 40 ways. He has also emphasised the difficulty in identifying corrupt officials. In the Mughal regime and during the British colonial rule, the traditions of giving *nazrana*, *shukrana* and gifts during various occasions to senior officials were in vogue. It promoted a culture of permissiveness in governance. In the initial years of independence, the political leaders were extremely concerned about corruption and mentioned it on several occasions in public speeches. The levels of corruption, however, continued to increase with economy of shortages and societal indifference to it. Santhanam Committee was appointed by the government to study this issue and make recommendation. It made extensive suggestions on handling corruption at all levels based on which a Central Vigilance Commission (CVC) was set up in 1964.

Many other recommendations about prescribing ethical norms and procedures to be adopted when complaints were received against ministers were not implemented.

The pre-reforms period had a large number of cases of corruption due to poor governance in delivery of public services, supply shortages, licence permit *raj*, export-import transactions and defence procurement. The post-reforms challenges have come from corruption in distribution of natural resources like spectrum, coal, defence purchases, award of projects and major construction contracts. The quality of governance in delivery of public services has shown very little change. The corruption has led to increase in the size of black money economy and flight of capital. The measurement of corruption by international organisations however indicates that corruption in India during the last 15 years has remained almost at the same level in terms of the World Bank Index and has slightly reduced in terms of TI Index. The 2005 TI study found bribes of $4.3 billion being given in 11 services at state level. Some others estimate it at about $14 billion. We feel these estimates are not unreasonable.

Efforts to Control Corruption in India

The main organisation to control corruption and evolve policies on it in central government is the CVC set up in 1964. In December 2013, Parliament passed the Lokpal Act but it has still not come into operation and appointment of Lokpals is yet to be finalised. The investigation of important corruption cases is taken up by Central Bureau of Investigation (CBI), an organisation set up under the Delhi Special Police Establishment (DSPE) Act 1946.[6] States have appointed Lokayuktas who look at corruption in the state government machinery. Seventeen states have passed laws on this. The courts have directed fair CBI investigation in several important cases involving powerful politicians or senior civil servants and monitor progress in several such cases. This has helped development of an environment of independent investigation. The government has also passed Right to Information (RTI) Act 2005 to improve transparency in its functioning. This will help in reducing corruption. The Whistle Blower Protection Bill 2011 was also passed this year to ensure protection to upright and honest civil servants for public disclosure made by them.[7] A number of states have also passed laws to improve delivery of public services.[8] The central bill on right of citizens for time-bound delivery of goods and services and redressal of their grievances, however, has still not become a law.

The use of technology has expanded gradually to improve the governance system and reduce corruption. With the launch of scheme for e-governance in 27 areas, a number of projects were taken up. Of these, MCA-21 and passport services have been completed and helped improved governance. Similarly, the railway reservation system and net banking have led to better quality of services. Development of Aadhar Card is an important instrument for delivery of public services. The common service centres set up as a result of e-governance plan, development of optical fibre network and scheme to connect all *panchayats* will improve connectivity and effective delivery of public services.[9]

India has several strong institutions of governance including an independent powerful media. These institutions include Election Commission, Comptroller and Auditor General (CAG), an independent judiciary with Supreme Court and High Court at the apex. These are constitutional offices with safeguards for independent functioning. The CAG reports on Bofors gun purchase, 2G spectrum allocations and coal block allocation reflect the independence of this office. The Chief Election Commissioner (CEC) conducts elections (parliament and legislatures) in accordance with the required time schedule and in a fair and independent manner. It has also taken measures to reduce corruption in electoral process by strengthening provisions of model code of conduct. The code prescribes norms of conduct for political parties and for candidates during elections. The Commission has also suggested measures for reforms in the electoral process. It is well recognised that actual expenditure in the election far exceeds the prescribed limits. Election financing is a major cause of corruption.

The New Strategy

The measures taken by the government are deficient in many areas. Poor health of several governance institutions particularly police and lower judiciary, lack of community participation, inadequate systemic reforms, weak political will and absence of independent agency to investigate and prosecute powerful politicians are some of these. Slow pace of electoral reforms and poor participation of women in governance have weakened anti-corruption efforts. Large political corruption has generated an atmosphere of tolerance of corrupt acts and provided an alibi to corrupt officials for indulging in corruption. An effective strategy is needed to promote a more honest society in the country.

The strategy to fight corruption should have four components: focus on economic growth, systemic and institutional reforms for prevention of corrupt acts, community education and its participation in fighting corruption, and effective implementation of anti-corruption law with suggested amendments. The entire strategy should revolve around economic growth. It helps evolution of an improved eco-system and development of new institutions of governance. With higher incomes, salaries of civil servants can be increased which may reduce their greed for corrupt practices. Growth acceleration requires increased private investment. Systems should be evolved for transparent and fair distribution of natural resources which may be required to be given to private investors. It has to be realised that we cannot price these resources at exorbitant levels as these are inputs in telecom, power, steel production, cement and fertilisers. The policy should be evolved keeping the pricing of these outputs. The pricing should not only be competitive *vis-à-vis* the international markets but should also ensure that the domestic market is sustainable in terms of price of the inputs.. Global experience shows that corruption goes down sharply as countries increase their incomes beyond $4,000. We can attain this level by 2025-2030, if GDP growth of 8 per cent can be sustained over the next decade.

The systemic and institutional reforms need extensive policy intervention. This will require Lokpal in the centre and Lokayukta in the states to discuss with various ministries, departments and organisations engaged in delivery of public service and public goods about the changes required in current systems, procedures, regulations and laws to have easy or corruption-free delivery. For this purpose, effective use of IT (information technology) should be made. They should develop a time-bound programme for ensuring corruption-free delivery of public services. The reforms will have to be based on trust of citizens rather than Inspector Raj. It may imply self-certification, accepting group verifications and extensive use of Aadhar Card. Wherever necessary, several private sector outlets and post offices can be used to provide new points of delivery of services. In the US, it is possible to give passports requests in any of the post offices. We should expand the functions of some of these institutions. The procedures should be tested periodically for assessing the quality of service. The accountability of public servants for successful implementation of these measures would have to be clearly spelt out. What is most important is ensuring corruption-free delivery by simplifying procedures.

To strengthen independence of institutions of governance, the selection process of CAG, CEC and ECs should be transparent. The suggestion made by ARC to have a committee chaired by PM including leader of opposition and representative of Chief Justice of India, Deputy Chairman of Rajya Sabha and the Speaker of Lok Sabha for selecting CEC should be accepted. We would suggest the same committee to select CAG too.

Some important causes of corruption in our political system are use of unethical practices for financing of political activities, growing number of MPs and MLAs with criminal records, weak anti-defection law and poor representation of women in the parliament and state legislatures. There is a need for a reform in the electoral process. Corruption in fighting of elections can be curbed by state funding of elections. A policy on this will need to be evolved. One possible norm can be a grant based on number of members of the political party and the votes polled by it in the election. For new political parties and candidates, a separate dispensation can be added. One can think of several other norms for such funding. The important point is to ensure acceptance and early implementation of this policy. Similarly, the suggestion to debar politicians from fighting elections for a period of three years or acquittal, whichever is earlier, against whom serious cases of crimes like rape, murder or dacoity are pending in the court should be implemented. Separate courts need to be set up to try offences related to such functionaries.

The law on defection has been extremely insufficient to control defection. It may be amended to provide that no defection be permitted for three years. It will ensure stability of governments and reduce horse trading. The participation of women in governance is still inadequate. Studies have shown that women are less tolerant of corruption than men. The law needs to be amended to ensure that every political party has at least one-third women candidates in elections to the parliament and state legislatures. We must plan for at least this share of our women in the parliament and state legislatures by 2030. A number of other systemic reforms will need to be taken based on the suggestions which may be made by the Lokpal and the Lokayukta. These should cover police, judiciary, economic institutions and *panchayats*.

The ethical values are an important part of any anti-corruption strategy. It is necessary to prescribe ethical norms for ministers, MPs and Members of State Legislature and to notify it for information of all citizens. An important ethical norm should be full financial disclosure of assets. Implementation of such values should be monitored by an ethics committee of the house and an independent commission on ethics set up by the Prime Minister. In addition, the Lokpal and Lokayukta should also monitor this. As part of the good ethical practices, acceptance or giving of gifts to officials and public servants should be completely banned, except on ceremonial occasions or where given by relations to each other. Any gift with commercial value received by an official should be sent to the government. The onus for proving that it was not given to him in official capacity should lie on the public servant concerned.

Community education is a critical component of the anti-corruption strategy. Societies have widely varying moral values and numbers of customs and traditions have developed over the centuries. A campaign in the media with use of television, radio, lectures by experts and inspirational messages should be undertaken by the Lokpal and Lokayukta for community education. These efforts should continue round the year and not be one-off thing. The whole exercise should be done as a national campaign and backed by the advisory groups set up in each organisation to get ideas and people participation.

Corruption prevention and education can only succeed if the machinery for investigation of corrupt cases is fair, independent and quick. The system for investigation needs to be reformed with the Lokpal being in charge of the entire process. The Lokpal Act 2013 has been passed and needs to come into force immediately. In the coming years, the Act will however need some changes to make investigations more independent. For this purpose, the Central Vigilance Commission and the CBI anti-corruption wing would need to be placed under Lokpal. To ensure checks and balance, the prosecution of these cases would then be done by the government. For this purpose, special counsels may be appointed by the government on recommendation of Attorney General (AG) in consultation with Lokpal. The result of investigations after the Lokpal has taken a decision on sanctioning prosecution or not agreeing to it in all cases, would be sent to the AG or special public prosecutors appointed for prosecuting corruption cases. They will then prosecute such cases. The courts will, after the charge sheets are filed or closure report given and based on material on record or such other material it may decide to get, decide whether to drop the case and accept the final report or frame charges. The above approach will enable fair investigation and not concentrate too much power in hands of the Lokpal. A similar approach should be adopted in the states where Lokayuktas may be in charge of anti-corruption cases.

The Lokpal and the Lokayukta must develop their own investigation wings in a period of five years and stop taking people from other sources including police. In the long run, this will ensure independence of the investigating agency. For any advice on any specialised matters, they could develop alternative sources. Such a mechanism could be in the form of an advisory group or technical experts co-opted for specific purposes.

The anti-corruption strategy must be so framed as to ensure that by 2030, the level of corruption in India may go down drastically. We should accelerate economic growth, have a high quality of life, and become a transparent and honest society in the next two decades.

Notes and References

1. For example, in the UK, the Bribery Act 2010 was introduced to update and enhance UK law on bribery including foreign bribery in order to address better the requirements of the 1997 OECD Anti-bribery Convention. It is now among the strictest legislation internationally on bribery. Notably, it introduces a new strict liability offence for companies and partnerships of failing to prevent bribers. Details are available at: *http://www.legislation.gov.uk/ukpga/2010/23/contents*. Similarly, the Foreign Corrupt Practices Act of 1977 (FCPA) is a United States Federal Law known primarily for two of its main provisions; one that addresses accounting transparency requirements under the Securities Exchanges Act of 1934 and another concerning bribery of foreign officials. Details are available at: *http://www.justice.gov/criminal/fraud/fcpa/*

2. United Nations (2004) "Practical Anti-corruption Measures for Prosecutors and Investigators", Chapter 2 in *United Nations Handbook on Corruption.*

3. The Prevention of Corruption Act, 1988 (No. 49 of 1988), is an Act of the Parliament of India enacted to combat corruption in government agencies and public sector businesses in India. Details are available at: *http://cbi.nic.in/rt_infoact/pcact.pdf.*

4. Mauro, P. (1995). "Corruption and Growth", *The Quarterly Journal of Economics* 110(3): 681–712. MIT Press. See also: Dreher, Axel and Thomas Herzfeld (2005). "The Economic Costs of Corruption: A Survey and New Evidence", *Public Economics* 0506001. EconWPA. Available at SSRN: *http://ssrn.com/abstract=734184 or http://dx.doi.org/10.2139/ssrn.734184*

5. World Bank (2012). *World Bank Development Indicators.* available at: *http://data.worldbank.org/data-catalog/world-development-indicators*

6. The CBI traces its origin to the Special Police Establishment (SPE) which was set up in 1941 by the Government of India (GoI). The functions of the SPE then were to investigate cases of bribery and corruption in transactions with the War & Supply Department. Of India during World War II and even after the end of the War, the need for a central government agency to investigate cases of bribery and corruption by Central Government employees was felt. The Delhi Special Police Establishment Act was therefore brought into force in 1946. The CBI's power to investigate cases is derived from this Act. Details available at: *www.cbi.nic.in.*

7. The Whistle Blowers Protection Act, 2011, is an Act of the Parliament of India which provides a mechanism to investigate alleged corruption and misuse of power by public servants and also protect anyone who exposes alleged wrongdoing in government bodies, projects and offices. The wrongdoing might take the form of fraud, corruption or mismanagement. The Act will also ensure punishment for false or frivolous complaints. The Act was approved by the Cabinet of India as part of a drive to eliminate corruption in the country's bureaucracy and passed by the Lok Sabha on 27 December 2011. The Bill was passed by Rajya Sabha on 21 February 2014 and received the President's assent on 9 May 2014. The Act has not come into force till now.

8. Right to Public Services legislation in India comprises statutory laws which guarantee time-bound delivery of services for various public services rendered by the government to citizens and provides mechanism for punishing the errant public servant who is deficient in providing the service stipulated under the statute. Right to Service legislation is meant to reduce corruption among the government officials and to increase transparency and public accountability. Madhya Pradesh became the first state in India to enact Right to Service Act on 18 August 2010 and Bihar was the second to enact this bill on 25 July 2011. Several other states like Bihar, Delhi, Punjab, Rajasthan, Himachal Pradesh, Kerala, Uttarakhand, Haryana, Uttar Pradesh and Jharkhand have introduced similar legislation on right to service to the citizen (as on April 2014).

9. The Ministry of Corporate Affairs (MCA), GoI, has initiated the MCA-21 project, which enables easy and secure access to MCA services in an assisted manner for corporate entities, professionals and general public. The MCA-21project is designed to fully automate all processes related to enforcement and compliance of the legal requirements under the Companies Act, 1956. The project further seeks to achieve inter-operability with the National e-Governance Services Delivery Gateway (NSDG) which will help extend MCA services to businesses via multiple front-end delivery channels, and which will also help provide other value-added services over and above the base services offered by MCA-21. For more information, details are available at: *http://www.mca.gov.in*.

Selected Bibliography

Ackerman, Susan R. (1999). *Corruption and Government: Causes Consequences and Reforms.* Cambridge University Press.

Agarwal, U.C. (2011). "Corruption Prevention: Need for Effective and Rational Approach", *Indian Journal of Public Administration* 57: 381-82.

Aizenman, J. and R. Glick (2003). "Military Expenditure, Threats, and Growth", *NBER Working Papers* 9618. National Bureau of Economic Research Inc.

Anderson, J., D. Kaufmann and F. Recanatini (2003). "Service Delivery, Poverty and Corruption: Common Threads from Diagnostic Surveys", Background paper for *World Development Report 2004.* Washington DC: World Bank. June 27. *www.worldbank.org/wbi/governance/capacitybuild/d-surveys.html*

Bai, J., S. Jayachandran, Edmund J. Malesky and Benjamin A. Olken (2013). "Does Economic Growth Reduce Corruption? Theory and Evidence from Vietnam", *NBER Working Papers* 19483. National Bureau of Economic Research, Inc.

Bardhan, P. (1997). "Corruption and Development: A Review of Issues", *Journal of Economic Literature* 35(3): 1320-46, September. American Economic Association.

Brunetti, A. and B. Weder (2003). "A Free Press is Bad News for Corruption", *Journal of Public Economics* 87: 1801-24.

Burroughs, Catherine (2000). *Women in British Romantic Theatre Drama: Performance and Society, 1790-1840.* Cambridge University Press. p.104.

Chew, David C.E. (1993). "Civil Service Pay in the Asian-Pacific Region", *Asian Pacific Economic Literature* 7(1).

Chowdhury, S.K. (2004). "The Effect of Democracy and Press Freedom on Corruption: An Empirical Test", *Economics Letters* 85: 93-101.

Clark, K. (1996). "Do We Have Enough Ethics in Governance Yet? An Answer from Fiduciary Theory", *U. ILL. L. REV.* 57.

Crain, Andrew D. (2014). *The Ford Presidency: A History.* McFarland Publishers.

Debroy, B. and L. Bhandari (2012). *Corruption in India: The DNA and RNA.* Konark Publications. pp.162-63.

Dollar, David, Raymond Fisman and Roberta Gatti (2001). "Are Women Really the Fairer Sex? Corruption and Women in Government",*Journal of Economic Behavior & Organization* 46(4): 423-29.

Dreher, A., C. Kotsogiannis and S. McCorriston (2007). "Corruption around the World: Evidence from a Structural Model", *Journal of Comparative Economics* 35: 443-66.

Dreher, Axel and Thomas Herzfeld (2005). "The Economic Costs of Corruption: A Survey and New Evidence", *Public Economics* 0506001. EconWPA. Available at SSRN: *http://ssrn.com/abstract=734184 or http://dx.doi.org/10.2139/ssrn.734184*

E&Y (2013). Survey on Bribery and Corruption: Ground Reality in India. Available at: *http://www.ey.com/Publication/vwLUAssets/Bribery_and_corruption:_ground_reality_in_India/$FILE/EY-FIDS-Bribery-and-corruption-ground-reality-in-India.pdf* (accessed on Sep 6, 2014).

Gill, S.S. (1998). *The Pathology of Corruption*. New Delhi: Harper Collins.

Grossman, Mark (2003). *Political Corruption in America: An Encyclopedia of Scandals, Power and Greed, Political Corruption in America: An Encyclopedia of Scandals, Power, and Greed*. Vol. 1. Grey House Publishing.

Guhan, S. and P. Samuel (1997). *Corruption in India: Agenda*. New Delhi: Vision Books Publication.

Gunnar, Myrdal (1968). *Asian Drama: An Inquiry into the Poverty of Nations*. 3 vols. Allen Lane: The Penguin Press. pp.702-03.

Gyimah-Brempong, K. (2002). "Corruption, Economic Growth, and Income Inequality in Africa", *Economics of Governance* 3: 183–209.

Halayya, M. (1985). *Corruption in India*. New Delhi: Affiliated East-West Press.

Hartung., William D. (2010). *Prophets of War: Lockheed Martin and the Making of Military-Industrial Complex*. Nation Books.

Heckelman, Jac C. and Benjamin Powell (2008). "Corruption and the Institutional Environment for Growth"', *Research Working Paper* 2008-6. Suffolk University.

———. (2010). "Corruption and the Institutional Environment for Growth", *Comparative Economic Studies* 52(3): 351-78, September. Palgrave Macmillan.

Heidenheimer, Arnold J. and Michael Johnston (eds) (2001). *Political Corruption: Concepts and Contexts*. Transaction Publishers. 3rd edition.

Houstan, Douglas A. (2007). "Can Corruption Ever Improve an Economy?", *Cato Journal* 27(3): 325-42.

Huntington, Samuel P. (1968). *Political Order in Changing Societies*. New Haven: Yale University Press.

Hunziker, S. and I. Kamimura (1996). *Kakuei Tanaka: A Political Biography of Modern Japan*. Cavendish Square Publishing.

Kangle, R.P. (1965). *The Kautiliya Arthashastra* (Part I-III). New Delhi: Motilal Banarsidas Publishers.

KPMG (2011). *Survey on Bribery and Corruption: Impact on Economy and Business Environment*. Available at: *http://www.kpmg.com/IN/en/IssuesAndInsights/ThoughtLeadership/KPMG_Bribery_Survey_Report_new.pdf* (accessed on Sep 6, 2014).

Leff, Nathaniel H. (1964). "'Economic Development through Bureaucratic Corruption", *The American Behavioral Scientist* 8(2): 8-14, November.

Lienert, I. (1998). "Civil Service Reform in Africa: Mixed results after 10 Years", *Finance and Development* 35(2).

Mauro, P. (1995). "Corruption and Growth", *The Quarterly Journal of Economics* 110(3): 681–712. MIT Press.

———. (1997). *The Effect of Corruption on Growth, Investment and Government Expenditure: A Cross-Country Analysis*. Corruption and the Global Economy. Institute of International Economics.

Mauzy, Dinae K. and R.S. Milne (2002). *Singapore Politics Under People Action Party.* London: Routledge Publication.

Meagher, P. (2004). "'Anti-corruption Agencies: A Review of Experience", *Discussion Papers on Institutions and Development* No. 04/02. Maryland: Center for Institutional Reform and the Informal Sector (IRIS Center), University of Maryland.

Mo, Pak Hung (2000). "Income Inequality and Economic Growth", *Kyklos* 53(3): 293–316.

Myrdal, Gunnar (1968). *Asian Drama: An Inquiry into the Poverty of Nations.* 3 Vols. Allen Lane: The Penguin Press.

———. (1970). "Corruption as a Hindrance to Modernization in South Asia", in Arnold J. Heidenheimer (ed.), *Political Corruption: Reading in Comparative Analysis.* New York: Holt, Rinehart & Winston. p.230.

Paton, H.J. (1979). *The Moral Law: Kant's Groundwork of The Metaphysic of Morals.* Bombay, Calcutta, Delhi, Madras: B. I. Publications.

Pellegrini L. and R. Gerlagh (2004). "Corruption's Effect on Growth and its Transmission Channels", *Kyklos* 57(3): 429-56.

Perotti, Roberto (1994). "Income Distribution and Investment", *European Econ. Rev.* 38(3): 827–35.

Quah, Jon S.T. (1999). "Corruption in Asian Countries: Can it be Minimized?" in *Public Administration Review* 59(6).

Quinton, A. (1973). *Utilitarian Ethics.* London: Macmillan Publications.

Rijckeghem, Caroline Van and Beatrice Weder (1997). "Corruption and the Rate of Temptation: Do Low Wages in the Civil Service Cause Corruption?", *IMF Working Paper.* Available at: *http://www.imf.org/external/pubs/ft/wp/wp9773.pdf* (Accessed on Sept. 3, 2014).

Rich, Ben R. and Leo Janos (1994). *Skunk Works: A Personal Memoir of My Years at Lockheed.* New York: Little Brown & Co.p.10.

Rock, M.T. and H. Bonnett (2004). "The Comparative Politics of Corruption: Accounting for the East Asian Paradox in Empirical Studies of Corruption, Growth and Investment", *World Development* 32(6): 999-1017.

Rose-Ackerman, S. (1999). *Corruption and Government: Causes, Consequences and Reform.* Cambridge University Press. p.27.

Russell, Jenniffer (2012). "E-Governance and Corruption in the States: Can Technology Help the Aam Admi", *Economic & Political Weekly* XIVII(25): 77.

Svensson J. (2005). "Eight Questions About Corruption", *Journal of Economic Perspectives* 19(3): 19-42.

Shleifer, A. and R.W. Vishny (1993). "Corruption", *Quarterly Journal of Economics* 108 (3): 599-617.

Strate, J.M., C.J. Parrish, C.D. Elder and C. Ford III (1989). "Life Span Civic Development and Voting Participation", *American Political Science Review* 83(2): 443-64.

Suphachalasai, S. (2005). "Bureaucratic Corruption and Mass Media", *Environmental Economy and Policy Research, Discussion Paper Series* Number 05.2005. University of Cambridge.

Swamy, A., Stephen Knack, Y. Lee and Omar Azfar (2000). "Gender and Corruption", *CDE Working Paper Series.* MA, USA: Centre for Development Economics, Williams College.

Tanzi, V. and Hamid R. Davoodi (2000). "Corruption, Growth, and Public Finances", *IMF Working Paper* WP/00/182.

Treisman, D. (2000). "The Causes of Corruption: A Cross-national Study", *Journal of Public Economics* 76: 399-457.

United Nations (2004) "Practical Anti-corruption Measures for Prosecutors and Investigators", Chapter 2 in *United Nations Handbook on Corruption.*

Vogl, F. (1999). "Curbing Corruption: The Media's Work. Recommendations for Action", *Transparency International Working Paper*. Presented at the 9th IACC.

Wade, Robert (1982). "Corruption: Where Does the Money Go?", *Economic and Political Weekly* 37(40).

Wei, S.–J. (2000). "How Taxing is Corruption on International Investors", *Review of Economics and Statistics* LXXXII(1): 1-11.

Wittgenstein, L. (1973). *Philosophical Investigations.* 3rd edition. Pearson Publication.

World Bank (1999). *The Hashemite Kingdom of Jordan: Public Sector Review.* Report No. 19664-JO. September 22. Social and Economic Development Group, Middle East and North Africa Region.

———. (2012). *World Bank Development Indicators.* available at: *http://data.worldbank.org/data-catalog/world-development-indicators.*

Documents

CAG Report No. 7 of 2012-13 for the period ended March 2012, *Performance Audit of Allocation of Coal Blocks and Augmentation of Coal Production* (Ministry of Coal), available at: *www.cag.gov.in*

Economic Survey, 2013-14, available at: *http://indiabudget.nic.in/survey.asp*

European Commission's Anti-Corruption Report (2014). Brussels, 3.2.2014 COM (2014) 38, Annex 26. It's available at: *http://formin.finland.fi/public/download.aspx?ID=100254&GUID=%7B4E90D9A4-B5EE-4EB9-B823-CCA228632695%7D (accessed on 29 August, 2014).*

OECD Publication on *Public Sector Integrity: A Framework for Assessment*. It's available at: *http://www.integriteitoverheid.nl/fileadmin/BIOS/data/Publicaties/Downloads/OECD_Publication_Public_Sector_Integrity_-_a_framework_for_assesment.pdf* (accessed on 29 August, 2014).

Stanford Encyclopedia of Philosophy, available at: *http://plato.stanford.edu/entries/corruption/*

The Prevention of Corruption Act, 1988 (No. 49 of 1988) is an Act of the Parliament of India enacted to combat corruption in government agencies and public sector businesses in India. Details are available at: *http://cbi.nic.in/rt_infoact/pcact.pdf*